Speak, Listen, and Learn

Building speaking, discussion, and presentation skills in every classroom

Colleen Abbott / Sally Godinho

Pembroke Publishers Limited

Pembroke Publishers
538 Hood Road
Markham, Ontario, Canada L3R 3K9
www.pembrokepublishers.com

Distributed in the U.S. by Stenhouse Publishers
477 Congress Street
Portland, ME 04101
www.stenhouse.com

This edition is adapted from a book originally titled *Thinking Voices*,
published in 2001 in Australia by Curriculum Corporation —
www.curriculum.edu.au

We acknowledge the financial support of the Government of Canada
through the Book Publishing Industry Development Program (BPIDP) for
our publishing activities.

We acknowledge the Government of Ontario through the Ontario Media
Development Corporation's Ontario Book Initiative.

Library and Archives Canada Cataloguing in Publication

Abbott, Colleen
   Speak, listen & learn : building speaking, discussion and presentation
skills in your classroom/Colleen Abbott, Sally Godinho ; [edited by] Cathy
Miyata.

Includes index.
ISBN 1-55138-177-X

   1. Oral communication—Study and teaching (Elementary) 2.
Listening—Study and teaching (Elementary) I. Godinho, Sally II. Miyata,
Cathy
III. Title.

LB1139.L3A23 2004   372.62'2 C2004-903663-7

Editor: Nancy Christoffer, Ronél Redman
Cover Design: John Zehethofer
Cover Artwork: Catherine Squared Pty. Ltd.
Design: Catherine Squared Pty. Ltd., JayTee Graphics

Printed and bound in Canada

9 8 7 6 5 4 3 2 1

Contents

Foreword   5
Introduction   7
Perspectives Underpinning the Text   7
How the Text Works   10

Unit 1 Tuning In—Speakers and Listeners   12
Active Listening   13
   Hearing Ears   13
   What Was the Message?   14
   Hearing Between the Lines   15
Informative Listening   16
   Follow Me   16
   Finding the Right Solution   17
   I Say You Said   18
   Experts   19
Engaging in Dialogue—Student Interaction   20
   Mapping Our Talk   20
   Sharing Talk-time   22
   Exploring Reasons   23
   Step by Step   24
Collaborating   25
   Role Switch   25
   This Is Not a Conversation!   26
   Consensus   28
Developing Questioning Strategies   29
   Asking in Class   29
   Seek and Find   30
Clarifying Meaning   31
   Oh, No!   31
   What's All That Stuff?   32
Unit 1 Student Profile   33

Unit 2 Tell Me the Story—Stories and Storytellers   34
Narrative Frameworks   35
   Telling Your Own Fairy Stories   35
   Modern Versions of Fairy Stories   37
   Personal Stories   38
Strategies for Engaging the Audience   40
   Readers' Theatre   40
   The Town Crier   41
   Chairs in Pairs   42
   Shorts (30-second or one-minute presentations)   43
   Using a Storyboard   44
   Let Me Tell You a Story   45
   Telling the Poem   47
Unit 2 Student Profile   48

Unit 3 So What's New?—Broadcasters   49
Broadcasting—Structural Organization   50
   Can You Identify?   50
   Viewing the News   52
   Same News Item, Different Story   54

Awareness of Context, Audience, and Purpose   55

   Speaking the Part   55

Questions and Interviews   56

   Identifying and Using Good Questions   56

   Designing the Questions   57

Fact or Opinion?   58

   Talk-back Radio   58

Using the Skills   59

   Student Reporters   59

   Creating News Stories from Pictures   60

Broadcasting Assessment Task   61

   Radio Programs   61

Unit 3 Student Profile   63

Unit 4 Let Me Change Your Mind—Many Points of View   64

Personal Opinion/Point of View   65

   Explaining My Position   65

   Presenting and Contesting Points of View   66

   "What We Believe"—Using Supportive
     Arguments   67

   Justifying an Action   68

Many Sides to the Argument   69

   Arguments For and Against   69

   The Panel   70

Challenging a Point of View   71

   When to Disagree   71

   What Do I Assume?   72

Persuasive Talk   73

   Analyzing Advertisements   73

Debating   74

   Getting the Facts   74

Unit 4 Student Profile   75

Resource Bank   76

Unit at a Glance   77

Teacher Checklist for Establishing a Collaborative
   Classroom   81

Checklist for Effective Communication   82

Group Assessment Sheet   83

Framework of Questions for Planning a Task   84

Student–Student Interaction   85

Let Me Tell You a Story Assessment Sheet   86

Observations of Presenters   87

Radio Program Assessment—Mandatory Roles   88

Radio Program Assessment—Negotiable Roles   89

Advertising Technique Chart   90

Structure of a Debate   91

Voting Criteria for a Debate   92

Glossary   93

Selected Bibliography   94

Index   95

Foreword

While in teacher's college (many years ago), my professor told my class to watch two movies—*The Prime of Miss Jean Brodie* and *Conrac*. Both movies featured the roles of teachers. I found the assignment rather odd at the time, as the teachers in both movies were eventually fired from their positions. I even asked my professor why he assigned these particular films. He laughed and admitted that the teachers portrayed were hardly ideal role models, but he hoped that we would recognize the passion the teachers had for their students. Passion. An admirable quality, to be sure, but clearly not the only thing we needed be good teachers? Unlike the "movie teachers" we would need skills to balance the passion. Hollywood was not the answer . . . or was it?

A few years later I viewed yet another "teacher movie," this one entitled *Up the Down Staircase*. In this film the teacher had passion and skill, but she also had an even more important ability. She knew how to impassion her students. I clearly remember one scene in which the teacher enticed her students into a lively discussion. Suddenly objections and declarations were bouncing across the room like errant tennis balls from one student to another, catapulting the students out of their apathy and into challenging one another about their ideas and beliefs. The students were on their feet, for perhaps the first time, with something to say. The students were the zealots and the teacher was quietly thrilled. Now this was my idea of a great teacher, whether it was Hollywood or not.

Speak, Listen, and Learn is the modern guide for educators who wish to become the kind of teacher from *Up the Down Staircase*. In this book you will find passion, the skill to balance the passion, and, most importantly, the means to impassion the students themselves. One flagstone after another is laid out neatly and precisely, leading us through the forest of student insecurities and fears and into the clearing of insight and self-confidence. The authors recognize not only the importance of developing communication skills, but the dire need for it to be engaging, challenging, and useful.

How many books have been written for teachers with lesson plan after lesson plan that instruct teachers to "discuss" a topic or theme with their students, but do not list the skills of discussion? Here at last is a strategic guide helping students to understand the subtle but significant manifestations of our language such as justification, implied meaning, opinion, persuasion, and argument.

Using Lev Vygotsky's theory of constructivist education, which enables students to build their own knowledge from opportunities in learning, Colleen Abbott and Sally Godinho have created a text that extensively explores the true nature of collaborative inquiry. Students will learn to respect and rely on each other for stimulating ideas, thought-provoking suggestions, and meaningful insights. As well, students are expected to consider not only *what* they are thinking, but *why* they are thinking it, and every lesson is concluded with a student reflection that will develop both academic and personal growth. The development, however, does not end with the students. This text also empowers educators to act as reflective practicers as well as facilitators, moderators, supporters, and role models in effective communication. Examples of questions to ask, steps to take, and things to look for are carefully laid out and easy to follow. Even questionings skills are addressed and will be improved if put into practice.

This book makes me want to seek out a Grade six classroom and watch what happens when the students are empowered to effectively discuss, collaborate, tell stories, broadcast, and debate. Reading this book has renewed my hope for a future generation of thinking, reflective listeners and speakers who can formulate an opinion, work cooperatively, and even facilitate with sensitivity. Education is key to a bright and improved future, and *Speak, Listen, and Learn* will help us achieve this great goal.

Cathy Miyata
Author of *Speaking Rules!*

Introduction

It is a talkative age. Just listen: cell phones, discussion groups, meetings, assemblies, forums, conferences, seminars, summits, talk-back radio, TV talk shows, and debates. In a world driven by the power of information technology, oral language continues to be our primary mode of communication.

Both our personal and professional lives are dependent on our ability to communicate effectively in different situational and social contexts. Good communicators have acquired effective speaking and listening skills, which include: selecting appropriate language, initiating talk, listening actively, focusing on meaning, sharing the speaking turns, asking questions, using appropriate body language, and sustaining the interest of the listener. They also understand the importance of collaborative inquiry, that is, sharing and exploring ideas through dialogue to enhance their own understanding of an issue or a concept.

The development of effective speaking and listening skills is basic to successful learning in all areas of school life and plays a central role in students becoming discriminating, thoughtful, and confident young adults. Educators have a responsibility to ensure that students have many opportunities to develop and refine their oral communication so that they will lead more fulfilling and meaningful lives.

Oral communication is central to all key learning areas. Despite acknowledgment of the importance of oral communication, the development of basic skills is frequently overlooked because of the priority given to the written mode, the overcrowded curriculum, etc. The four units in *Speak, Listen, and Learn* provide a range of activities that are designed to actively engage students in developing their speaking and listening skills. Minimal preparation time is required of teachers, and the activities can be integrated with other subjects, topics, and themes.

Perspectives Underpinning the Text

The four units are based on the constructivist perspective that for effective learning to take place students need opportunities to construct their own knowledge. A constructivist approach involves students synthesizing new experiences with what they have previously come to understand. It requires teachers to focus their practice on teaching for understanding rather than transmitting specific knowledge to students. Students are encouraged to do the thinking and the talking; the teacher's role is to scaffold their learning by:

- modelling the skills associated with an activity;
- probing students' understanding;
- focusing students' thinking;
- extending students' ideas through questioning and prompts;
- giving constructive feedback; and
- guiding students to reflect on their own learning.

Exploratory talk

In a constructivist classroom students are encouraged to explore meaning by thinking out loud. Teachers need to be mindful that exploratory talk often sounds tentative, fragmented, and confused because it captures students thinking in action. False starts, changes of direction, hesitations, and re-phrasings are to be expected as the students work to shape their ideas.

Metacognition

Metacognition is sometimes referred to as "thinking about thinking," and involves students developing awareness and control over their own thinking. Talking about the learning process— that is, what they know, what they don't know, and wondering why they are doing what they are doing—is an essential link in the transfer of knowledge. Each activity in this text requires students to monitor and assess the learning that has taken place, and time is allocated for some individual or collaborative reflection.

Collaborative inquiry

Collaborative inquiry underpins all the activities. Inquiry does not take place when students simply state their point of view or recount an experience. Rather, it takes place when students are interacting with one another's ideas, examining how those ideas are formed and whether they are reasonable or not.

The collaborative inquiry process is about sharing ideas that are fundamental to thinking, particularly cooperative, self-corrective thinking. It requires students to think about what they are discussing and, also, their ways of thinking. The process encourages students to learn skills that enable them to explore, develop, monitor, and adjust their thinking and talking in cooperation with others. When students are involved in learning through collaborative inquiry they make their ideas accessible to one another and demonstrate they are prepared to change and develop. Students learn to respect themselves and others, even when they have different ways of thinking and making meaning, thus building self-confidence and self-knowledge.

Collaborative inquiry demands that speaking and listening focus on content that is problematic in some way. It does not have to be a debate or a contest, but rather an exploration of ideas and meaning. The stimulus and content of discussion must be both relevant and challenging. Students are interested in big issues that affect them, such as fairness, justice, truth, and power—not just issues to do with the environment and the school. Student ownership of the collaborative inquiry process is essential.

The importance of developing effective discussion skills

Students are frequently required to participate in small-group or whole-class discussions. Yet, often the strategies and the skills that discussion entails are overlooked. Consequently, students are unaware that discussion is a distinct form of talk that involves collaborative inquiry and interactive dialogue.

Discussion is different from conversation in that it focuses on a particular issue or a concern and is not open to the participants changing the topic as they wish. Students who are familiar with the discussion process and the skills involved are more likely to feel confident in their ability to share different ideas and opinions. The following characteristics are true of collaborative inquiry, and provide a guideline for what teachers should encourage in class discussions:

Reflectiveness — showing reflective insights into the discussion process

Responsiveness — responding with sensitivity to the ideas and opinions of others

Diversity — voicing different opinions on an issue

Clarity — searching for clarity in the expression of meaning

Evidence — providing reasons and evidence to support arguments

Consistency — considering coherence and consistency of thoughts and arguments

Flexibility — keeping an open mind and being prepared to change one's mind in light of new information

Risk taking — willingness to explore tentative, unformed ideas.

The role of the teacher

According to Santi (1993), the teacher should take on a number of roles to support the discussion process, and to demonstrate effective discussion skills to students:

- **Facilitator**: helps the circulation and comprehension of ideas so students see themselves as problem seekers and problem solvers; for example, "Lou, how might you explain the phrase *power corrupts*?"

- **Provoker**: stimulates participants to explore and deepen their own positions; for example, "Was that statement you made about theft based on evidence?"

- **Modulator**: leads the reasoning process in the most productive directions; for example, "How could we follow up on Jan's point?"

- **Monitor**: controls the correctness of the reasoning; for example, "Isn't that an assumption about that group?"

- **Supporter**: supports and encourages the cognitive operations involved in the thinking process; for example, "That's an interesting point of view. Can anyone think of a different approach?"

Modelling facilitation

The modelling of effective speaking and listening skills by teachers is pivotal in shaping students' communicative talk. Through talking and interacting with students, teachers are able to lead students to new levels of conceptual understanding. Teachers facilitate students' learning by scaffolding their engagement in the activities and guiding them to construct their own knowledge. Students and teachers work collaboratively to acquire new understandings and to achieve specific learning outcomes. The following statements summarize important aspects of a teacher's role as model and facilitator:

- The creation of a supportive, caring environment is fundamental to the role of facilitation.

- Teachers must facilitate the inquiry process rather than dominate it.

- Teachers need to articulate and model the skills and thinking required for successful collaborative inquiry. This requires them to explain their own thinking processes, develop skilful questioning strategies, and use self-corrective statements when necessary.

- The extent to which the teacher is able to demonstrate respect for and genuine interest in the ideas and thought processes of the students has a very real impact on the positive learning culture of the class.

- Good facilitation requires collaboration, intervention, and participation.

- Teachers must model questions that ask for clarification and elaboration of ideas; for example:

  Am I right in thinking that you mean . . .?

  Can you give me some further evidence?

  What is the source of that information?

  Why do you accept this source as reasonable?

  Can you explain that in more detail?

  What assumptions might you be making about . . .?

- Part of the role of the teacher as facilitator is to draw the students' attention to what is happening in the discussion, and to provide time for them to reflect and comment on this process.

- It is not the role of the teacher to respond to every student. In a collaborative inquiry the students are encouraged to respond to each other, and their responses can be turned back to the group for comment.

How the Text Works

The text is divided into four units.

1. Tuning In concentrates on developing individual and small-group communication skills that are used in later units.

2. Tell Me the Story explores narrative frameworks and strategies for engaging the audience.

3. So What's New? develops performance and presentation skills.

4. Let Me Change Your Mind explores ways of developing and contesting points of view.

Each unit follows a similar structure:

- practical activities which include a stated purpose, practical guidelines for implementation, ideas for extension, and recommendations for teacher and student reflection on learning; and

- an activity for evaluating student learning, with an accompanying evaluation checklist.

Areas within the classroom will need to be created where speaking and listening skills can be explored and practised independently and collaboratively. The skills and strategies covered in each lesson need to be made explicit to students, and teachers are encouraged to make ongoing assessment of students' progress.

Assessment and evaluation

Teacher and student assessment is an integral part of each activity. Student assessment can take three different forms: self-assessment, peer/small-group assessment and whole-class assessment.

The benefits associated with student assessment include:

- improved reflection and greater student ownership of the learning;
- self-identification of learning needs, enabling students to set personal goals; and
- development of a positive attitude towards assessment procedures.

A reproducible Checklist for Effective Communication is provided for student use on page 82. It highlights some key points that students need to consider when reflecting on their speaking and listening. Students should be encouraged to add to the list.

A reproducible Group Assessment Sheet is provided on page 83 for assessment of group discussion, and reflective stems are provided after each activity to guide students' self-assessment.

The reflective stems and questions presented at the end of each lesson also offer support for teachers in their assessment of the learning that has occurred, the effectiveness of the lesson procedure, and consideration of any follow-up that may be needed. The Teacher Checklist for Establishing a Collaborative Classroom on page 81 should be used regularly for reflection on the facilitation of discussion.

A template for recording individual student profiles is provided at the end of each unit to assist evaluation.

Unit 1

Tuning In—

Speakers and Listeners

Understanding the give-and-take relationship between speakers and listeners is crucial in the development of communication skills. Students need to be aware of the variety of roles they will undertake in this relationship, and they deserve opportunities to develop proficiency in those roles. The activities in Unit 1 develop the awareness and skills students need to become effective listeners and speakers as individuals and in small groups. These activities form the foundation blocks for the activities introduced in the following units.

Consider the six abilities developed in the Unit 1: Active Listening, Informative Listening, Engaging in Dialogue, Collaborating, Developing Questioning Strategies, and Clarifying Meaning. Do your students have strengths or weaknesses in any of these areas? Ask yourself questions like: *Do students really listen to each other? Can they follow instructions? Can they collaborate enough to reach a consensus? Do they understand how to effectively brainstorm?* Based on your assessment, select the activities needed. Your students might need one or two of the activities, or they might need all of them. Keep in mind, however, the activities in this unit support and underpin all of the other units, so give students time to explore and feel comfortable with the skills presented. When your students have a working proficiency of these skills, move on to Unit 2.

Hearing Ears

ACTIVE LISTENING

The purpose of this activity is to explore what we hear and what we remember, and to improve aural memory.

Activity

1. Ask students to sketch the outline of a head in the centre of a landscape piece of paper. Students will later be required to write in the space to the left and right of their picture, as well as inside the head itself (see sample below).

2. Explain that you will read some information and students are to record what they hear inside the head. Begin with a short piece or list of words so that initial success is guaranteed.

3. Write the full text on the board. Students copy this on the left side of the page.

4. On the right side of the page students write the words that they did not record on the first hearing.

5. Discuss what was not heard and why. Ask students to share the strategies they use when trying to hear and remember.

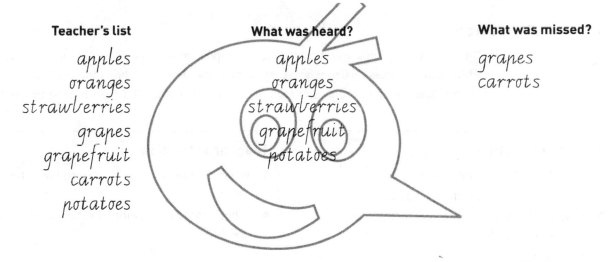

Teacher's list	What was heard?	What was missed?
apples	apples	grapes
oranges	oranges	carrots
strawberries	strawberries	
grapes	grapefruit	
grapefruit	potatoes	
carrots		
potatoes		

Extension/Variation

This activity can be used on a regular basis to build students' aural memory.

Student reflection

- I was surprised that I was able to remember so many/so few words. Why did this happen?
- This activity could help me improve my memory for . . . (for example, spelling, taking notes).

Teacher reflection

- Identify the students who would benefit from further practice in aural memory skills.
- Plan some follow-up activities where you could use this strategy, for example, for spelling or story telling.

ACTIVE LISTENING

What Was the Message?

The purpose of this activity is to develop skill in listening for detail using recorded messages, and to develop the ability to record messages.

Activity

1. Use the PMI strategy (positive, minus, and interesting points—see Glossary) to brainstorm the class's experiences with listening to recorded messages and leaving recorded messages.

2. Develop guidelines for recording information contained in recorded messages. Use the following questions to focus the listening: *Who is speaking? What is the time? What are the important details of the message? What is the return phone number? What other action is required?* (These guidelines may also be used for leaving messages.)

3. Prepare simple taped messages, and play them while students write down the information.

4. Pair students to check what was recorded. Discuss any variations.

5. Have pairs of students prepare and record messages. Play their messages to the class and check against the guidelines.

Extension/Variation

Pairs of students prepare and record more complex messages which either include irrelevant detail or omit necessary detail, and play them to the class. The class should be aware that the new messages include irrelevant detail or omit necessary detail. Check against the guidelines.

Student reflection

- Something I found easy was . . .
- Something I found difficult was . . .
- To what degree has this activity helped to build my confidence . . .?

Teacher reflection

- What further practice is required in listening for detail?
- Where can opportunities for further practice be created?

ACTIVE LISTENING

Hearing Between the Lines

The purpose of this activity is to explore implied meaning in relation to varying audiences, contexts, and intentions.

Activity

1. Explain the meaning of the expression "reading between the lines"—when people read between the lines they construct meaning that is implied rather than stated.

2. Facilitate class discussion about the different meanings people may make when they hear the same words, that is, meaning that is implied rather than stated. Use expressions that may have different meanings; for example, "wicked," or questions such as: How was school today? How was your weekend? (Such questions may mean different things when asked by a parent, student, or a friend.)

3. In pairs, have students explore implied meaning using tone of voice, facial expression, and posture. One student selects a statement and says it to his or her partner. The partner explains his or her analysis of the implied meaning. Sample statements:

   Nice hair cut.

   I did well on my exam.

   I really like your shoes.

   Are you going out tonight?

   That was wicked.

   Is your mother going to be home?

   I need some food.

4. When sufficient examples have been provided, ask students to reflect on the reasons why meanings are different. Consider, for example, meanings that vary depending on age groups or cultural groups, the purpose of the speaker, and the intention of the hearer.

Extension/Variation

A small group of students may collect examples of expressions used in different contexts where it is common to find a variety of meanings, such as the home, advertising, school, and share these with the class.

Student reflection

- Something new that I learned from this discussion is . . .
- Reasons why people create different meanings from the same words are . . .

Teacher reflection

- To what extent did students explore the reasons why we make different meanings?
- How effectively did they interact with each other's ideas?

INFORMATIVE
LISTENING

Follow Me

The purpose of this activity is to practise giving detailed instructions and listening to direction.

Activity

1. Students work in partners. The first partner creates a pattern or a structural formation from construction kit pieces, such as Lego. The second partner cannot see the design.

2. Partner one instructs partner two on how to replicate the design by giving clear, explicit instructions. When the replicated design is completed, the partners switch roles.

3. As a class, facilitate a discussion on which role was easier and why.

4. Ask students to suggest strategies that helped them in both roles. List strategies on chart paper for future reference.

5. Throughout the term, have students repeat the activity several times, with different partners. Ask students to assess whether or not they are improving in their ability to give and follow instructions.

Extension/Variation

Appoint students to give instructions to the entire class. These instructions could be a math puzzle, construction activity, computer program task, or a recipe.

Student reflection

- I was surprised that I preferred the . . . role. It made me feel . . .
- This activity could help me improve my ability to . . .

Teacher reflection

- Identify students who would benefit from further practise in giving and taking instructions.
- Plan some follow up activities that incorporate some of the strategies suggested by the students.

INFORMATIVE LISTENING

Finding the Right Solution

The purpose of this activity is to allow small groups to explore how to sort and order their ideas.

Activity

1. Arrange students in small groups. Assign each group a problem to solve. Problems could be school based, curriculum related, current affairs, or hypothetical situations.

2. Instruct students to brainstorm solutions.

   Rules for brainstorming:
   - all suggestions are accepted no matter how far-fetched;
   - no discouraging of answers through negative reactions (rolling eyes, moaning, laughing);
   - students may piggy back and/or elaborate on each other's ideas; and
   - time limit is imposed

3. After brainstorming is complete, groups rank their ideas in order of worth or usefulness.

4. Groups share their top three solutions with the rest of the class, justifying their ranking.

Extension/Variation

Repeat this exercise as a creative writing exercise.

Student reflection

- I discovered that more ideas were generated when . . .
- I could use this exercise when I am . . .

Teacher reflection

- What further practice is required in brainstorming?
- What further practice is required in prioritizing?
- How can I rearrange the groups to further enhance these skills?

I Say You Said

The purpose of this activity is to listen in order to summarize key points.

Activity

1. Students should work in pairs. Each pair is assigned a topic or issue to discuss. Topics can be school based, curriculum related, or based on current affairs. For example, Children under the age of 17 should be tried in adult court if the crime is serious.

2. Give students five minutes to discuss their views on the issue. Remind students to share equal talk-time. Partners listen carefully, questioning when necessary to seek clarification or elaboration of what has been said. Warn students that they will have to remember what their partner said. Students may use questions like: *Why do you feel that way? Can you elaborate or explain that comment? Did you ever feel differently about this?*

3. When time limit has been reached, end the talk-time and ask students to consider three points their partner made that they felt were interesting and/or important. If they need to, they may ask one last question of their partner to clarify a point.

4. Pairs join to form a group of four. Students take turns to summarize for the group the views held by their partners. They should be able to restate at least three points.

5. As a class, discuss the following questions:
   - *Did you feel the key points restated were the key points you made?*
   - *Who had the most responsibility to decide which were the key points, the speaker or the listener/summarizer?*
   - *What strategies did you use to remember key points?*

These can be listed and posted for future use.

Extension/Variation

- Assign one student to summarize the opinions of the whole group.
- Repeat this activity experimenting with different strategies for summarizing.

Student reflection

- I was uncomfortable when . . .
- I was pleased when . . .
- When I was summarizing I remembered only certain points because . . .

Teacher reflection

- How well did the partners listen to each other?
- Do students understand how to summarize what they have heard?

Experts

The purpose of this activity is to practise summarizing information and to experience reporting the information gathered.

Activity

1. Divide students into groups of six. Call these groups the foundation groups. Number students in the foundation groups from 1 to 6. All students with the same number now leave their foundation group and form expert groups.

2. Give each expert group an aspect of a topic. For example, deforestation, air pollution, water pollution, erosion, and land clearing are all aspects of an environmental study. Give the expert groups a limited time to collate information they have on the topic.

3. The experts return to their foundation groups and report their expert groups' findings.

4. As a class, discuss strategies used to summarize and report effectively. List suggestions and post for future reference.

Extension/Variation

● Repeat this activity several times, adjusting the groups and the topic. Advise students to experiment with some of the strategies listed and discuss why or why not they worked for them.

● This also works well when introducing a new curriculum of study, to uncover what the students already know.

Student reflection

● I found the summarizing exercise . . . because . . .
● I found the reporting exercise . . . because . . .
● Next time I will try . . .

Teacher reflection

● Note the skill level demonstrated for both summarizing and reporting. Which students will need more experience in these areas?

Mapping Our Talk

ENGAGING IN DIALOGUE— STUDENT INTERACTION

The purpose of this activity is to allow small groups to identify their communication patterns, and to develop some strategies to use in small-group discussion.

Teacher preparation

Copies of the blank sociogram, Student–Student Interaction, for students to complete (see page 85).

Activity

1. Ask students to suggest some of the positive and the negative aspects of small-group discussions. For example, it is interesting to hear the ideas of others; students talk over the top of each other; one person sometimes dominates the talk.

2. Explain that a sociogram is a way of recording and monitoring communication patterns. Show the sample sociogram provided on the following page and ask what it reveals about the group's communication patterns. For example, why might Mehemed have no arrows? Stress that group interaction is the responsibility of all members. When a student does not participate, it usually reflects on the group's interactive skills.

3. Brainstorm issues for discussion from current class themes or topics of interest. Remember that for a discussion to occur there needs to be contested positions where students have different points of view.

4. Working in small groups, select a topic for a short discussion (3–5 minutes) during which communication patterns are recorded on the blank sociogram supplied. Explain that the group must decide their position on the issue. Choose a student in each group to record the talk-turns.

5. At the end of the discussion, the groups discuss their communication patterns and consider how they could improve their interaction.

6. Ask students to suggest some strategies that would assist small-group discussions. Make a class list to guide future discussions. This can be added to over time.

Extension/Variation

Tape the discussion and ask students to chart the talk patterns during the replay.

Student reflection

● Complete the Group Assessment Sheet on page 83.

Teacher reflection

● How did the interaction patterns vary between groups?

● What reasons might be behind the variance?

● To what extent did students shape their own strategies for small-group discussions?

Sample group interactive patterns

Recorder: Jess

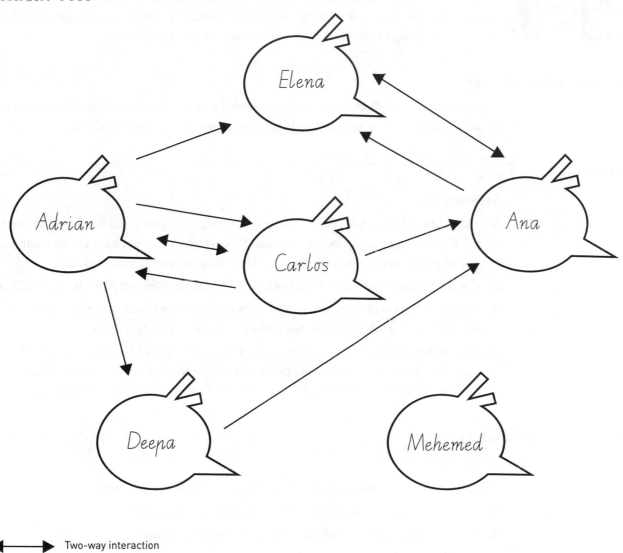

Two-way interaction
One-way interaction

Sharing Talk-time

This activity provides strategies for making students conscious of the need to share the talk-time between group members. Its purpose is to increase students' awareness that group members should be given equal opportunity to express their ideas and opinions.

Teacher preparation

Copies of a selected short story or poem for small-group discussions. (Several different stories or poems could be used so that the groups can swap to try the two strategies.)

Activity

Strategy 1

1. Ask students if they have ever experienced working in a group and felt they have not had a fair opportunity to contribute to the talk. Discuss why this might happen; for example, interruptions by peers and dominance of the discussion by several students.

2. Inform students that some strategies to address this problem are going to be practised.

3. Arrange students in small groups and distribute copies of the chosen pieces of literature. Tell students to read their piece silently and to mark their favorite section.

4. One student begins the discussion, explaining the reason for his or her selection. The speaker must then remain silent while the other members comment on the selection. The speaker has the last chance to reply before the student to the left of the speaker takes a turn.

Extension/Variation

Strategy 2

Materials: a symbolic microphone for the speaker to hold, and counters.

1. Rotate the literature pieces so that each group has a new piece.

2. Give each group a "microphone" and four counters per student.

3. Explain the rules for the discussion:
   - Students may only speak if they have been passed the "microphone."
   - The student holding the "microphone" chooses who may speak next.
   - Each time students talk, they must return a counter to the centre of the table. When all counters are returned, a student forfeits the right to talk and must wait for others to have the same number of speaking turns.

Student reflection
- Continuing to use these strategies would be useful/not useful because . . .

Teacher reflection
- How beneficial might it be for the class to continue one of the strategies tested?

ENGAGING IN DIALOGUE— STUDENT INTERACTION

Exploring Reasons

The purpose of this activity is to develop skills to engage in dialogue through questioning the reasons that underpin opinions.

Activity

1. Briefly explain that people have reasons for their opinions, but sometimes people do not explain them clearly to others or think them through.

2. As a warm-up, ask the class to suggest several different situations where students were asked to provide reasons for their opinions. Encourage students to be creative.

3. List responses to the question: *Why are we asked to give reasons?* For example, people are interested in what we think; they want to find out what we know; they want to be able to disagree/agree with us; they don't understand our ideas.

4. Model examples of how to ask for further information about reasons. Display these questions for easy reference:
   Where do you think your reason came from?
   When did you start to think that?
   Can you tell me why you think that?
   Is there another reason for your opinion?
   Can you see how that reason could be connected with another?
   Is there anything that could contradict your reason?
   If I suggested this as another reason for . . . how do you see that fits with your idea?

5. Provide a common opinion that most students will agree with, such as "Holidays are great." Students provide reasons for this opinion and are questioned by other students using the modelled questions. They could also use a follow-up "Why?" to gain further information.

6. Explain that your role is to facilitate the discussion by ensuring that everyone has a turn and that the dialogue is between the students. *Note*: When small groups use this process a student will take the facilitator's role.

Extension/Variation

In small groups students discuss more contentious opinions and use the question-based dialogue to explore reasoning. Students could explore the reasons why a character from literature held a particular opinion, or an opinion from a figure in the news.

Student reflection

● PMI: As a class, students list the positives, the minuses, and the interesting points involved in using the strategies (see Glossary).

Teacher reflection

● To what extent did students use the questions provided?

● Do they require further practice with engaging in dialogue about reasons for opinions?

● To what extent did students show respect for each other's ideas?

Step by Step

The purpose of this activity is to practise interaction with each other's ideas.

Activity

1. Model the process outlined below, using a well-known rhyme such as "Jack and Jill." Record ideas on the board so that the students do not have to rely on their memory.

2. Students should work in pairs. One student reads the first line aloud and then adds some information to it. The second student adds to the extra information provided by the first student before adding the next line and repeating the process (see sample below).

Student X: **Jack and Jill went up the hill**

Jill was a faster runner than Jack.

Student Y: Jack had a sore leg.

Student Y: **To fetch a pail of water.**

The pipes were blocked down below.

Student X: That happened at least once a week.

Student X: **Jack fell down and broke his crown.**

He was always falling over.

Student Y: Jill was always giving him a shove.

Student Y: **And Jill came tumbling after.**

Because she was round, she rolled more easily.

Students X: But she still didn't beat him down the hill.

3. When students understand the process they can prepare their own dialogue and read it aloud to the class. The class must listen to check that each student responded to the other's ideas.

4. Conclude with the student reflection (see below).

Extension/Variation

Students can use the same process with other, more complex texts.

Student reflection

● How difficult/easy was it to build on another student's response?

Teacher reflection

● How effectively did students listen for the new information, and add to it?

COLLABORATING

Role Switch

The purpose of this activity is to explore the roles and responsibilities within a group situation.

Activity

1. Ask students to brainstorm the roles of different people in a group situation. List the roles and the responsibilities.

2. Add to the list the following roles (if they have not already been mentioned).
   - **Leader:** clarifies the task; takes overall responsibility for completion of task
   - **Reporter:** is responsible for reporting the groups ideas to the class; often has to summarize and prioritize the ideas
   - **Timer:** monitors the use of time and keeps discussion moving
   - **Recorder:** keeps written notes of key points and ideas
   - **Encourager:** encourages full participation of all group members
   - **Designer:** is responsible for the visual presentation of ideas

3. Arrange students in small groups. Assign each student a role within the group. (Roles can be written on a slip of paper and pulled from a container.)

4. Assign a task to each group, which must be competed by a certain time; for example, create a game using a ruler, pencil, and paper clip. Begin timing the task, but after a couple of minutes, stop the action and instruct students to pass their role to the person on their left. Instruct groups to continue the task. Have students continue to change roles every few minutes, but do not let the task go on much longer than 15 minutes.

5. As a class, discuss how it felt to play the different roles and why. Poll which roles they enjoyed the most and the least.

Extension/Variation

Group work with assigned roles can be used regularly in all subjects where group work is useful. Reflect on the different roles experienced and build a list of strategies for each role that may be helpful to other students.

Student reflection

- I most enjoyed playing the role of . . . because . . .
- I least enjoyed playing the role of . . . because . . .
- Next time I would like to play the role of . . . and try to . . .

Teacher reflection

- Which roles did students find the easiest to implement and which ones the most difficult?
- How can I facilitate more experience and more comfort in the different roles?

This Is Not a Conversation!

The purpose of this activity is to explore the collaborative and interactive nature of a discussion.

Activity

1. Explain to the class that you will be comparing a conversation to a discussion. Invite two students to read the scripts aloud.

   Script 1
   A. I wish it would rain, it's so hot.
   B. Nah, if it rains we can't go skateboarding later.

   A. Hey, did you hear about what happened to Nancy Borden this morning in gym class?
   B. What? What?

   A. Broke her arm in two places.
   B. How?

   A. Tripped over the dodgeball.
   B. Ha ha! Let's go eat something, I'm starved.

   Script 2
   A. According to the Americans, Laura Secord is a traitor.
   B. Why would they think that?

   A. She was an American and she helped the British in the war. That makes her a traitor.
   B. Can a hero also be a traitor?

   A. Sure. A hero on one side is hardly a hero to the other side. It's a question of perspective.
   B. But what you just told me changes my perspective of Laura Secord. I don't think she's honorable any more. In my opinion she is not a hero at all.

2. Ask the class which script represents a conversation and which script represents a discussion. Ask students to justify their opinions.

3. Create a chart to list the characteristics of a conversation on one side and the characteristics of a discussion on the other side. Some characteristics of a conversation are: open ended, topic and focus can change at any time, can be personal or objective. Some characteristics of a discussion are: open-ended, focus and topic is fixed and should not change on a participant's whim, can be personal or objective.

4. Instruct students to point out similarities and differences between the two modes of communication.

5. Explain to the students that you are going to have a discussion. Post the following roles and responsibilities of the members of a discussion group:

   In a discussion the participants are expected to:
   - **Explore ideas:** involves risk taking and inquisitiveness
   - **Interact with others' ideas:** helps form new views and perspectives; involves open-mindedness and flexibility

- **Examine if the ideas work or are reasonable:** involves reflective thinking and responsiveness

In a discussion the facilitator has several roles and is expected to:

- **Act as facilitator:** involves encouraging the circulation and understanding of ideas
- **Act as provoker:** involves stimulating the participants to explore and deepen their positions
- **Act as monitor:** involves controlling the correctness of the participants' opinions

6. State that the discussion period will be limited (perhaps five minutes to start) and assign a student as timer. Ask the timer to give the class a one-minute warning so the discussion can wind down. Announce that you will act as the facilitator. Explain that a discussion is much more interesting and exciting if it is focused on something problematic, challenging, and/or relevant. State the topic of the discussion and open the discussion. (At this stage, your questioning and prompting techniques will be crucial in modelling effective facilitating. Suggested prompts and questions are listed in "the role of the teacher," see page 9.)

7. At the conclusion of the discussion, ask students to reflect on the expectations of the participants and the facilitator and decide if the expectations were met.

Extension/Variation

Repeat this activity many times, varying the length and topic of the discussions. Eventually, assign students as facilitators. At the conclusion of the discussions, list some of the pertinent questions that were posed by participants and facilitators that can be used again.

Student reflection

- I was encouraged to speak when the facilitator said . . .
- When I am the facilitator I will try to . . .
- As the participant, in the next discussion I will . . .

Teacher reflection

- To what extent did students engage in the discussion?
- How can I encourage even more participation?

Consensus

The purpose of this activity is to achieve a consensus while working as a group.

Activity

1. Explain to the students that they will be working on a group consensus assignment. While they work through their task, they should consider how a consensus task is similar to brainstorming strategies and discussion strategies and how it is different.

2. Establish the rules of consensus:
    - all group members must participate;
    - the opinion of every group member must be honored;
    - all members must eventually agree on final decisions; and
    - all members must be willing to bend and concede.

3. Arrange students in small groups. Assign each group a task to achieve within a time limit. These tasks can be creative; for example, design a costume for a new singing group. This initially involves the group making decisions about the music genre, audience age, and style of the group before trying to reach the consensus on the costume design.

4. When allotted time is over, bring groups together to discuss the following:

    How easily was the consensus reached?

    What did the group do when it reached an impasse?

    How was reaching a consensus similar to brainstorming and discussion strategies?

Extension/Variation

Repeat this activity with new groups and more challenging and practical tasks that involve responsibility; for example, create new games for play day, establish what each person's role will be in the execution of the game, and then let them run it.

Student reflection

- While working on a consensus I learned to . . .
- I will use this strategy in the future when I . . .

Teacher reflection

- How well did the group members work together?
- Were the same students bending to the will of other students? How can I redirect this pattern?

Asking in Class

The purpose of this activity is to develop confidence and skill to ask questions in class and establish a list of useful questioning strategies.

Activity

1. Ask students to suggest times when they need to ask questions in front of the class. List their responses on the board. For example, when I lose track of the lesson; when I need something that I have left at home; when I don't understand the instructions; when I don't know what to do next.

2. Share a personal experience that illustrates the emotions one might feel in a similar situation, for example, embarrassment, anxiety, or fear. Encourage students to share their experiences of these emotions.

3. Add to the list on the board if necessary.

4. Develop questions that could be used in the situations listed.

5. Record these questions on a large piece of paper and display in the room for future reference.

Sample situation and questions

Losing track of the lesson:

Q: I remember this part but . . . can you tell me what I missed, please?

Q: I understand this part . . . but can someone please help with . . . ?

Extension/Variation

- Ask students to list the negative and positive responses, when questions are asked in class. Negative responses might include looks, murmurs, or impatient responses. Positive responses might include nods, murmurs of agreement, and comments such as, "Yes, me too." or "That would be helpful."

- A small group of students can draw up questions to use in other public situations, such as meetings with older students or teachers, or in public places such as a library or a restaurant.

Student reflection

- This has helped me to . . .
- I will use this strategy when . . .

Teacher reflection

- This activity was of benefit to all/most/some/ a few of the class. Identify specific students who may benefit from this strategy. Note instances when they will be encouraged to use it.

Seek and Find

The purpose of this activity is to develop effective questioning strategies for seeking information in a public place. This activity involves role play.

Activity

1. Organize random groups of four or five students using a numbering-off method.

2. Explain that the random method helps us to work with people who are new to us, and that this activity is designed to help us develop skills used when dealing with people who are not well known to us.

3. Set the scene. Two members of the group are young people who are lost, while the others are adults the students may encounter. Suggest a number of places that are relevant to the students' experience; for example, in a large school, in the city, at a hockey game, at a concert, in a shopping centre, at the zoo.

4. Explain the task. Each group is to create and perform a short play that demonstrates the use of polite, relevant questions that may help the lost students gain the information they require from the adults.

5. Explain the rules. Only polite questions are answered. Adults must respond to the question but do not have to answer it fully or correctly. Adults can ask questions in return, which the lost students must answer.

6. Present the role plays and ask the audience to listen carefully and note whether the rules are obeyed.

7. Conclude with student reflection (see below).

Extension/Variation

Students can change the scene and adapt the rules. Have students role-play a student seeking information from a busy adult. The student must find the information by asking up to five different, polite questions. The adult must act aloof and preoccupied. The asker must persist in order to obtain the information. Eventually the adult must provide the information.

Student reflection

● I feel confident about asking questions in public because . . .

● The most effective question is . . . because . . .

Teacher reflection

● To what extent do students require further practice in effective questioning skills?

● Where can these strategies be incorporated into other key learning areas?

CLARIFYING MEANNG

Oh, No!

The purpose of this activity is to develop students' understanding of how different factors can influence the way people construct meaning.

Activity

1. Ask a student to come to the front of the class and repeat the phrase, "Oh, no!," expressing different feelings; for example, surprise, anger, fear, shock. The student should not state the feeling expressed until asked to.

2. Class members guess what feeling was expressed.

3. The student in front of the class questions the class members as to why they guessed a specific feeling. Possible answers: it reminded me of a situation; the look on your face; the tone of your voice.

4. Repeat the activity with different students using different expressions, such as "Hurry up," "Come on," and "All right."

5. In pairs, have students take turns exploring different expressions.

6. Discuss how this knowledge can make the students better public speakers.

Extension/Variation

- Repeat the activity but have the speaker turn their back to the class. Compare the results and highlight the importance of facial expression.

- Practise using other single words or simple phrases that make different meanings dependent upon the context in which they are expressed, for example, "Yes, please," "Help me," "Really", "Don't."

Student reflection

- Something I will remember and apply from this activity is . . .

Teacher reflection

- How successful was this activity in meeting the aims?

- What further activities should be planned?

What's All That Stuff?

The purpose of this activity is to develop awareness of the need to clarify the meaning of commonly used words and expressions and to explore how different people may make different meanings.

This activity could be used to assess most of the abilities addressed in this unit.

Activity

1. Brainstorm the situations when students use the expression "just stuff" in response to a question. Record on the board, for example, parental requests for information about what students have for homework, what they did when out with friends, or what may be in a bag they carry. Students should have many more suggestions as this is such a commonly used expression.

2. List the following questions on the board to stimulate discussion. Remind students of the need to listen and respond to each other's ideas.
   ● *What do you mean when you say "just stuff" in response to a question?*
   ● *What meaning do you expect the questioner to make of your answers?*
   ● *What meaning might the questioner actually make?*

3. Use a common question, for example: *What did you do over the weekend?* Change the questioner to a grandparent, a teacher, a friend.

4. Ask the students to frame some general statements about communicating meaning, using the following stems:
   ● When we communicate meaning we often find that . . .
   ● Words can mean different things . . .
   ● Some expressions have . . .
   ● Different situations can . . .

Extension/Variation

List and explore the possible meanings of other expressions commonly used by students such as "unreal," "deadly," "wicked," "sick."

Student reflection

● Students share what they have learned from the activity with a partner. Provide a stem if necessary, for example: I learnt that words can . . . Students record their responses on sheets of paper to be collected. Alternatively, the class can jointly construct some learning statements.

● At the conclusion of this assessment activity students will be able to complete most of the evaluation chart included at the end of the unit.

Teacher reflection

● Review and discuss the Student Profile assessment chart on page 33.

Student Profile

Name: _____ Date: _____

This chart lists the general skills and attitudes that you have been practising. For each skill, place an X in the column that you think best describes your progress.

Assessment criteria	Usually	Sometimes	Not yet
I listen for relevant detail.			
I think about what I am listening for.			
I can give and follow instructions.			
I listen and learn from others while brainstorming.			
I can link the meaning of one idea to another.			
I adjust what I am saying to suit my purpose.			
I acknowledge different points of view.			
I challenge other points of view appropriately.			
I provide support for my own ideas.			
I look for the reasons for my own ideas and for others' ideas.			
I actively participate in group work in a variety of roles.			
I engage in discussions.			
I collaborate when trying to reach a consensus.			
I ask questions to clarify meaning.			
I know that people make different meanings.			
I respect the ideas of other people.			

My strengths include: _____

_____

A new goal I have set for myself is: _____

_____

Something I have learned from this unit that has helped me is: _____

_____

Unit 2

Tell Me the Story—

Stories and Storytellers

The narrative, or story, is a powerful means of communication in the lives of both children and adults. Oral and written stories are told and heard within a social and cultural context. They shape the way people view both their immediate world and their wider world. Literature is steeped in narrative forms, such as stories, songs, traditional rhymes, myths, and legends, which are an integral part of children's early literacy experiences.

Narratives involve both story reading and story telling. Story reading relates to the written text, while story telling relates to the oral tradition. Most people engage in some form of story telling every day of their lives by conveying to others something they have seen, heard, or experienced. Through telling stories of their experiences, people create personal histories.

Story telling requires both the teller and the audience to create mental pictures from words, and involves interaction between the storyteller and the audience. Successful interaction is dependent on the storyteller engaging the audience through the use of voice, facial expression, and body language to heighten and embellish the meaning and mood of spoken words.

There are many ways to make the classroom a place where stories are loved and respected and where storytellers feel welcome and valued. Consider inviting members of the community into your classroom to share personal stories or having storytellers come share traditional stories. Students could bring in a valued object from home and tell a brief story about it, or they could research and tell the history of a family member.

In this unit, students have the opportunity to develop their skills of storying their own experiences, and story telling within a literature context. The unit also seeks to make students aware of the power of narrative to engage an audience, and to realize the pleasure involved in sharing stories.

Telling Your Own Fairy Stories

The purpose of this activity is to have students consider the traditional narrative structure of fairy stories, and to create their own fairy stories using this structure.

Activity

1. Ask students what features they associate with fairy stories, such as a happy ending, a moral, good characters, bad characters.

2. Brainstorm other types of narratives they may be familiar with, such as myths, legends, fables, rhymes, folk tales, fairy tales, real-life experiences, creative stories, fantasies, and adventure tales.

3. Discuss what is understood about the organizational structure of a traditional story (orientation, complication, a chronological sequence of events, resolution).

4. Use the traditional framework (see sample below) to record the structure of some well-known fairy stories.

Beginning	
Orientation:	
● setting	Countryside
● characters	Mother, three little pigs, wolf
● introduction of problem	Mother sends pigs out into the world
Middle	
Complication	Wolf wants to eat pigs
Sequence of events	1. Pigs build houses of straw, wood, and bricks.
	2. Wolf blows down houses of straw and wood. Pigs escape.
	3. Pigs plan to kill wolf.
	4. Wolf falls down chimney and dies.
End	
Resolution/moral of the story	Plan and take time to do things properly.

5. Explain that as preparation for creating their own fairy stories, the class is going to brainstorm some common associations with these stories using the following headings. (Students may like to suggest additional ideas as headings.)

   ● **Characters**: good characters such as handsome princes, beautiful princesses, young children, fairy godmothers; bad characters such as wicked witches, dragons, foxes, wolves, toads

   ● **Family members**: stepmother, spiteful stepsisters, missing or deceased mothers, bossy or weak fathers

- **Settings and homes**: forest, woods, castle, cottage, toadstool house, pumpkin house, gingerbread house
- **Plots**: children who become lost, frogs that turn into princes, sleeping princesses, cruel adults, or beasts who harm innocent children
- **Special accessories**: coaches, magic carpets, broomsticks, wishing wells, pumpkin carriages, magic beans, spells. A good reference point is *The Fairy Catalogue: All you need to make a fairy story* by Sally Gardner.

6. In small groups, students create their own fairy stories using a traditional narrative structure.

7. Each group shares the story it has created.

8. Ask students to consider in what ways the stories were stereotyped. They should consider the characters, the roles the characters played, the outcomes for the characters, the language they used. Discuss how important students consider the issue of stereotyping to be in these stories.

Extension/Variation

Have students prepare role plays of their stories. These could then be presented to students in younger grades.

Student reflection

Complete the Group Assessment Sheet on page 83.

or

Reflective stems:

- When creating a traditional narrative, the important points to remember are . . .
- What do I like/dislike about the traditional narrative structure?

Teacher reflection

- How effectively did this activity develop students' understanding of traditional narrative structure?
- How well developed is the students' understanding of the concept of stereotyping?

Modern Versions of Fairy Stories

The purpose of this activity is to consider the linguistic structures and features of a traditional narrative. Each group requires a copy of a traditional fairy story.

Activity

1. Invite students to recall favorite traditional stories they were read or told in their early childhood years. Ask students to recall what they particularly liked about the stories and why they liked having them retold.

2. Read the class a traditional story, such as "Jack and the Beanstalk."

3. Ask students to identify some of the language features they associate with traditional fairy stories, such as words that signal the beginning and the ending, the use of repetition, a predictable structure, a moral to the story. Then ask the students to consider how the characters, settings, and language in "Jack and the Beanstalk" might be different if written today. For example, Jack might be a computer expert, an environmentalist, a political activist, and the setting could be a rural town, a city apartment block, an inner suburban residence.

4. Have the students share their responses to the modern version.

5. Divide the students into small groups and give each group a traditional story to read. Ask the students to prepare a retelling of their story in a current-day context. Encourage changes to the setting, characters, and language, but explain that the linguistic structures and features associated with traditional stories must be retained. For instance, their story must keep the traditional structure of orientation, complication, and resolution. The language features should include a traditional beginning such as "Once upon a time" and a traditional ending such as "They all lived happily ever after."

6. Each group presents their retelling.

7. Discuss:
   - what was lost or gained by the changes;
   - which versions were preferred; and
   - why children continue to enjoy having stories read or told in their traditional format.

Extension/Variation

- Encourage students from various cultures to share their favorite traditional stories.
- Read and discuss some modern versions of traditional stories.

Student reflection

- Features that I identify with a traditional fairy story are . . .
- What I like/dislike about traditional fairy stories is . . .

Teacher reflection

- What did the activity reveal about students' understanding of the linguistic structures and features of traditional stories?
- Which features did students find the most difficult to identify?

NARRATIVE
FRAMEWORKS

Personal Stories

The purpose of this activity is to increase students' awareness that sharing an experience with others involves story telling, and that stories are part of personal history. This is an ongoing activity that involves students being offered the opportunity to practise telling personal anecdotes to the class.

Activity

1. Ask the class to recall when someone (a friend, a relative, a visitor to the school) told them a personal story that really engaged their interest. Probe what they found so engaging about the story and the way it was told (use of humor, suspense, surprise twist).

2. Tell the class a personal story that is comfortable to share, such as an embarrassing experience or a dramatic event.
   - Start the story with the WHO (who was there) and the WHERE (where it happened), so the listener gets a mental image.
   - Add the WHEN if the story happened a long time ago, so the picture of you changes in their head.
   - Explain the WHAT or the action (what you were doing at the time).
   - Build up to the climax, the moment of embarrassment, or injury, or fear.
   - Tell how the story resolved itself.

   Post these steps on a chart so students can follow the sequence.

3. Brainstorm some weekly themes for personal stories; for example: My best holiday; An unforgettable experience; An embarrassing situation. Stagger the telling of stories over a week.

4. Explain that each week students will be asked to share a personal story on the theme decided. Set a time limit of two minutes for stories. Suggest students bring a prop to add some visual impact to the talk.

5. Discuss what points students need to remember when giving a talk. For example:
   - Have an effective opening and closing.
   - Tell events in a logical sequence.
   - Use cue cards, if needed, to stay on track.
   - Speak clearly, and do not rush.
   - Vary the tone of your voice.
   - Use appropriate language.
   - Remain on the topic.
   - Make eye contact with the audience.
   - Use a visual aid if appropriate.
   - Rehearse your talk with the family.

   Compile a class checklist.

6. At the end of each week discuss:

- the way that telling a personal story helped students to make meaning from an experience; and
- the two best stories of the week and the group's reason for their choice.

Extension/Variation

Record students telling their personal stories on tape or video and discuss their story telling techniques.

Student reflection

- Important points I need to remember when telling a story are . . .
- Something I did well when I told my story was . . .
- Something I need to improve is . . .

Teacher reflection

- Which skills from the checklist require the most attention?
- What opportunities can I provide to ensure these skills are consolidated?

STRATEGIES FOR ENGAGING THE AUDIENCE

Readers' Theatre

The purpose of this activity is to practise performance skills, including audience involvement. The activity requires two timeslots: one to write the scripts; and the other to rehearse and present the stories.

Activity

1. Ask students to recall storytellers who have engaged the students' participation in the storytelling process. Have them recall how this was done.

Storyteller/setting	Story	Student engagement
Prep teacher	"The Three Little Pigs"	Recite the repeated lines of the text.
Theatre	"Peter and the Wolf"	Hiss and boo when the wolf appears.

2. In small groups, have students select an appropriate and familiar story or poem to present as Readers' Theatre to younger students. Explain that some audience participation is required, and suggest that stories or poems that provide opportunities for repetition are useful for this purpose.

3. Brief the students that the script will require some modification of the original text because Readers' Theatre focuses on dialogue. Explain how direct speech can replace indirect speech (see Glossary). Suggest that a narrator can provide key background details and prompt audience participation. Have the students prepare a script that includes audience involvement.

4. Stress the importance of the volume, pace, pitch, and intonation in the delivery of words. Revise the definition of these words (see Glossary).

5. Allow time for students to rehearse.

6. Each group presents its story to a junior class.

7. After the presentations, discuss:
   - the role of audience participation in holding young children's interest; and
   - variations or improvements the students might introduce if repeating the experience.

Extension/Variation

Create rap versions of stories for older students.

Student reflection
- Complete the Group Assessment Sheet on page 83.

Teacher reflection
- What aspects of the students' reading aloud need further development?
- How effectively did students' engage the audience in their presentations?
- To what extent did students own the discussion?

STRATEGIES FOR ENGAGING THE AUDIENCE

The Town Crier

The purpose of this group of activities is for students to practise engaging the audience, using eye contact, and using varying aspects of their voices such as volume, pace, pitch, stress, and intonation (see Glossary for definitions).

Activity

1. Explain that the original Town Criers were among the first journalists. Their job was to pass on information.

2. Discuss the features of the environment in which the Town Criers had to work: noise, movement, and activities in the street.

3. List the strategies that Town Criers used to get their messages across: short phrases, powerful words, loud and dramatic voices, change of volume, pace, and pitch.

4. Each student selects a short piece of news and takes on the role of the Class Crier.

5. Have one presentation each morning and encourage the students to project their voices as if in a noisy street.

Extension/Variation

- Class Criers could be used to announce school activities at assembly.
- Link this activity to a study of local or national news.

Student reflection

- Did I reach all ears?
- What was my most effective strategy?
- What area of my presentation needs more work?

Teacher reflection

- Note the students who require more practice in projecting their voice or varying their pitch and pace. Think of opportunities when these students could be given extra practice.

Chairs in Pairs

The purpose of this activity is to practise using body language and different tones of voice when attempting to convince others of a point of view.

Activity

1. Chairs are arranged in two circles, one circle inside the other. Pairs of students sit facing each other.

2. Explain the following: Students on the outside circle are to convince their partners on the inside circle that they should accompany them somewhere after school; for example, the mall, the park, a baseball diamond. The students on the inside chairs are supposed to go home to look after their younger sibling. The students on the outside circle must use an aggressive approach.

3. Students sitting on the outside have one minute to convince their partners.

4. Change the approach to flattery.

5. Move the outside students clockwise one chair, and change the approach to calm and logical.

6. Partners swap positions and the outside students move anticlockwise one place. Change the approach to one of temptation.

7. Change the scenario to one of student-choice; for example, sport, music, entertainment. Try other approaches as well, but keep the talking time short.

8. Conclude with student reflection (see below).

Extension/Variation

Two students act as observers and provide feedback about the successful use of voice, body language, and facial expressions they observed.

Student reflection

● I was nearly convinced by . . . because . . .
● An example of the way body language can be effectively used is . . .
● Something I learned about varying the tone of my voice is . . .

Teacher reflection

● Which strategies require further work?
● What activities can I provide to assist this?

Shorts (30-second or one-minute presentations)

A "short" is a brief timeframe—between 30 seconds and a minute—in which an event or anecdote is shared with the audience.

The purpose of this activity is to practise strategies used for successful presentations. These include: maintaining eye contact, controlling aspects of voice; adopting a comfortable, steady stance; presenting supportive evidence; using effective introductions and conclusions; and other techniques for gaining audience attention.

Activity

1. Brainstorm a list of strategies used by speakers to engage the audience. Students will be aware of many strategies, but ensure the list includes those stated in the purpose above. Explain that each student will have opportunities to present some shorts.

2. Have each student select two strategies to practise—for example, eye contact and voice expression—in the presentation of the short, *Something that Made Me Laugh/Cry*.

3. Set a regular time for presentations. Students should prepare their shorts as homework. Encourage students to rehearse. Before their presentation to the class, students state the strategies they have selected to practise.

4. After each topic, conclude with the student reflection (see below).

Possible titles for shorts

- A Favorite Poem
- You Wouldn't Believe This
- A Problem and Its Solution
- This Made Me Laugh
- Amazing but True (retelling a strange anecdote from the newspaper, or recounting an amazing personal experience)
- My Scariest Experience
- An Embarrassing Moment

Extension/Variation

Use the most successful presentations at assembly.

Student reflection

- My best strategies were . . .
- Those needing further development are . . .
- A goal I have set for my next presentation is . . .

Teacher reflection

- Note the strategies that need further development.
- How can opportunities be provided to develop these strategies?

Using a Storyboard

The use of storyboards can be extensive, such as ordering events in a report, developing a storyline, sequencing topics for a presentation, or focusing an audience on key ideas. They are particularly useful for those students who lack confidence in memory skills.

The purpose of this activity is to develop the skill of using a storyboard to support the telling of a story.

Activity

1. Discuss the structure of the storyboard, explaining its dual purpose—that it can act as a visual aid for the storyteller and as a prop for engaging the audience.

2. Model the use of a storyboard using a familiar story. To do this, state the six main events and write brief captions below them.

3. Select a particular unit of work where telling the story of the people or characters involved will be meaningful to the students' learning; for example, a character from the class novel, a famous scientist, an influential person from a current topic of study. Ask students to choose the story of the person they would like to put on their storyboard.

4. Students work in pairs to prepare storyboards.

5. Individual students present stories to the class.

6. Conclude with student reflection (see below).

Extension/Variation

Students could use a multimedia approach, such as a PowerPoint slide show or generating a stack using HyperStudio. These approaches could be used for the presentation of a project, research topic, or factual/descriptive report.

Student reflection

- The advantages and disadvantages of using a storyboard to assist in the preparation and telling of a story are . . .
- Other situations where I might use this strategy include . . .

Teacher reflection

- Identify the students who would benefit most from using storyboards as a learning tool.
- How could storyboards be used to scaffold learning in other key learning areas?

Let Me Tell You a Story

The purpose of this activity is to practise story telling as a performance and to develop an understanding that successful story telling requires rehearsal. It is recommended that students use myths, legends, or fables as their narrative basis, because they are relatively short and usually have a clearly identifiable narrative structure.

The activity introduces the role of the critical friend.

The role of a critical friend

A critical friend is a peer who assesses a presentation according to criteria negotiated by the presenter and the teacher. A good critical friend will be someone who is trusted, who understands what the student is trying to do, and who can suggest improvements without hurting the presenter's feelings.

Teacher preparation

The critical friend is given a copy of Let Me Tell You a Story Assessment Sheet on page 86. At the conclusion of each presentation, the critical friend and the presenter discuss the assessment in private and then return the sheet to the teacher.

Activity

1. Read a selection of legends, myths, or fables.

2. Have students recall other legends, myths, or fables that they have read or heard. Discuss the characteristics of these story forms.

3. Ask students to choose a favorite to share with the class. Explain the need to focus on the structure of the narrative (orientation, complication, sequence of events, and resolution) and some story-telling strategies to entertain the audience.

4. Explain that students will be negotiating areas for assessment with the teacher.

5. Discuss the role of critical friends. Either students or the teacher select the critical friends.

6. Students prepare a simple storyboard or notes on cue cards to assist with the memorization of the story. They may nominate which parts of the story will be emphasised and what strategies will be chosen to make it interesting to the audience. Students decide on how they want their audience to feel, and what strategies they will use to create that response, such as humor to relax the audience and a scary voice to create suspense and tension. The information is recorded on the assessment sheet and given to the teacher and critical friend.

7. Provide some time for the students to prepare and practise their stories. Practice should be done in pairs or groups of three so students become very familiar with their chosen stories. This activity is not a memory test.

8. Before students present their stories, inform the class of the strategies they have selected for assessment. Ask the class to provide constructive feedback on these strategies.

9. The presenters discuss the assessment with their critical friends.

Student reflection

- To what extent did the critical friend help me to assess my performance?
- How well did I achieve in the areas I set down for assessment?

Teacher reflection

- How effective was this activity work as an assessment task?
- To what extent did the students focus on the strategies they set for their assessment?
- Evaluate the role of the critical friend.

STRATEGIES FOR ENGAGING THE AUDIENCE

Telling the Poem

The purpose of this activity is threefold:

● to practise skills that entertain an audience with a group presentation of a narrative poem;

● to experiment with the use of sound, actions, and voice control which highlight the changing nature of the narrative; and

● to use the group's different talents and learning styles.

Activity

1. Prepare for this activity by reading several narrative poems to the class (see resource list below). Briefly explain that such poems usually follow a similar structure to a story book narrative.

2. Organize students into small groups. Randomly group or place different types of learners together so that each group has someone with the following strengths: verbal, musical, rhythmical, kinaesthetic, interpersonal, and visual.

3. Explain that the task is to prepare and present a performance of a narrative poem. The storyline should be supported by the creative use of sound, movement, and props. Exclude complex costumes and allow a minimum number of props. Limit sound effects to equipment available in the classroom. Encourage the use of multimedia.

4. Prepare copies of several poems. Allow groups to choose a poem. Keep poems reasonably short. Explain that the students can read the poems—they do not have to memorize them but will need to make good eye contact with the audience.

5. Allocate a specific time for preparation.

6. Groups present their poems to the class.

Some suggested poems:

Roald Dahl's Revolting Rhymes by Roald Dahl

The Owl and the Pussy Cat by Edward Lear

Custard the Dragon by Ogden Nash

James, James Morrison Morrison by A.A. Milne

The Highwayman by Alfred Noyes

Extension/Variation

● This activity can be refined for a presentation at assembly.

Student reflection

● Something good that I contributed to our group's presentation was . . .

● Something I need to remember when presenting a poem next time is . . .

Teacher reflection

● How appropriately did the groups use students' individual talents?

● Did the groups entertain the audience well?

● How effectively did the groups use sound, action, and voice control?

Student Profile

Name: _____ Date: _____

This chart lists the skills that you have been practising as storytellers. For each skill, place an X in the column that you think best describes your progress.

Assessment criteria	Usually	Sometimes	Not yet
I confidently tell my personal stories to the class.			
I sequence events logically when telling a story.			
I make eye contact with the audience when I speak.			
I appropriately adjust the volume of my voice.			
I vary the pitch of my voice.			
I control the pace of my talk (pausing, speeding up, slowing down).			
I use animated facial expressions and gestures.			
I have a comfortable, steady stance when speaking.			
I use effective techniques for focusing the audience's attention (multimedia, props).			
I contribute my special skills when story telling in groups.			
I respect the ideas of other people.			

Something I do well when I tell a story to an audience: _____

_____

A goal I have set to improve my story telling: _____

_____

A skill I have learned or improved through participation in this unit: _____

_____

Teacher's comments: _____

_____

Unit 3

So What's New?–

Broadcasters

New technologies mean that information can be transmitted globally by voice and at the touch of a key. In a world where each year the volume of information increases exponentially, the importance of communicating clearly and concisely is essential. Broadcasters—be they on radio, television, the Internet, or some other media outlet—know that the content of a report and its delivery style are critical features when conveying information to an audience.

In schools and in the workplace, there is an increasing emphasis on oral presentation and reporting. In both environments, information can be presented within a range of contexts, both formal and informal. While the purpose and context will vary, there are some basic skills that can assist students to structure and deliver information more effectively. This unit provides opportunities for students to develop these skills in a range of contexts.

The unit begins with some activities that reinforce the report genre and its associated language features. The performance-based activities presented later in the unit assume that students have an understanding of the organizational structure of reports. Activities cover the spectrum, from spontaneous talk to more polished, rehearsed talk. They include reflection and self-assessment strategies that encourage the students to examine the effectiveness of their communication.

Can You Identify?

The purpose of this activity is twofold: firstly, to identify the background information for a news story; and secondly, to identify the story's main idea and the supporting details.

Teacher preparation

A taped radio broadcast of the news.

Activity

1. Ask students what essential information needs to be provided in a news story. What are the questions that need to be answered? For example: *What happened? Who was involved? Where did it happen? When did it happen? Why did it happen?*

2. Using the focus questions, listen to a taped news story and record the essential information.

3. Ask students to recall the news story's main idea. From memory, ask students to recall the details that supported this idea. List these on the board.

4. Replay the tape, and ask students to check their responses, making any necessary alterations.

5. Demonstrate how to note down information as they listen, using the sample chart below. Complete the first item as a class. Make explicit that some information, such as the main point, can be filled in after the listening is completed. Then have students work individually or in pairs to fill in the information for other items.

6. Have students discuss some of the strategies they used to get the necessary information.

	Item 1	Item 2
Who?	Canadian Prime Minister and US President	New York Rangers vs Toronto Maple Leafs
What?	Meeting	Hockey game
Where?	Washington	Madison Square Garden
When?	Yesterday	Today
Why?	To develop a relationship	Semi-final
How?	Prime Minister flew in	Very close game
Main point	Leaders met	Rangers won
Supporting details	Doesn't happen often	Who scored goals
	Important for future	Number of spectators

Extension/Variation

Repeat the process with short newspaper articles. Talk about the different strategies used when reading and listening for information.

Student reflection

- The most challenging part of this activity was to identify . . .
- Something I need more practice with is . . .

Teacher reflection

- What degree of ease/difficulty did the class experience in identifying the background information, main point and the supporting ideas?

Viewing the News

The purpose of the activity is to explore different approaches to the news service used by the television stations. The activity may need to be spread over several days, as each group needs the opportunity to view their video.

Teacher preparation

Videotapes of different news broadcasts. (Students can take responsibility for the taping.)

Activity

1. Students suggest a preferred television news service and discuss reasons for their choice.

2. Group students and allocate a video to each group. Arrange viewing times.

3. Explain that each group is to prepare a three-minute report on their news service. Suggest that different group members take responsibility for different tasks.

4. Students should record their observations and use the information gathered to compile their reports. Discuss the requirements of the observation sheet by modelling the sample opposite.

5. Groups present their reports and a group evaluation of the news service. They should consider how informative the news service was and how effectively it engaged the audience.

6. Discuss the differences in presentation styles and how these are matched to the target audience.

Extension/Variation

Use radio news services and compare the differences in style and intended audiences.

Student reflection

● Things that are important when I watch the news are . . .

Teacher reflection

● How competently did students manage the note taking?

● To what extent did students recognize different approaches to news services?

News service	
Channel:	Seven
Time:	6:00 pm
Target audience	Family viewing
Presenter/s (name, gender, age, dress style, interaction with audience and other presenters)	● Jennifer Adams Female, age: 20s, smart white suit—business dress, warm smile but comments all focused on the news. ● Tim Watson Male, age: 30s, business suit, relaxed but serious.
News stories (in order of appearance)	● Fire devastates Western regions ● Tax problems with GST ● Federal election ● New medical breakthrough on diabetes ● Missing man found with amnesia ● World cup winners ● 'Smellovision'—US development
Other items included in the service (weather, sport, finance report, etc.)	● Sport: basketball update, golf tournament results, football training, and horse races. ● Weather: Canada-wide and details on Victoria's weather for next week.
Use of advertising	Two segments. Channel 7 programs, Plant World, The Handy Plumber, Extreme Car Care, Jumbo peanut butter, Flash sunglasses, Boat Safety, World Vision, All-clean toilet cleaner.
Use of graphics (maps, summaries, logos, etc.)	● Names of reporters and location of news stories ● Weather maps ● Channel 7 icon
Sound effects	News theme music at regular intervals

BROADCASTING—
STRUCTURAL
ORGANIZATION

Same News Item, Different Story

The purpose of this activity is to help students realize that news services can give different versions of the same news item.

Teacher preparation

- The news videos from "Viewing the News" (page 52) can be used to complete this activity.
- In advance, mark where the same news item occurs on the different tapes. (Students could take responsibility for this task.)

Activity

1. Students recall different versions of a news item they have viewed or heard through the media (newspapers, television, radio). Discuss why versions of the same event sometimes differ.

2. View the first video clip together. Students may wish to note some key points.

3. View a second video. Pause when students signal a difference they want to record. Repeat the process for each news item.

4. Prepare a chart with two columns headed Same and Different. Have the class record their observations.

5. Working in small groups, ask students to rank the news items in order of their preference. Explain that they will first have to decide on some criteria for judging the news items. Have students note the criteria they used for their ranking.

6. The groups share their decisions.

Extension/Variation

Use articles from different newspapers or magazines that cover the same event.

or

Listen to radio and television broadcasts of the same news items and compare how they are presented.

Student reflection

- Two reasons why the same story is sometimes told differently are . . .
- When ranking the stories, our group considered the following criteria . . .

Teacher reflection

- What understanding do students have of the reasons why a news item can be shaped differently by the media?
- How readily were the student groups able to reach consensus on the ranking of news items/articles?

54 So What's New?

Speaking the Part

AWARENESS OF CONTEXT, AUDIENCE, AND PURPOSE

The purpose of this activity is to make students aware of how television presenters adjust their voice and presentation style to match the audience and their subject matter. The activity involves the students viewing videotape extracts from a diverse range of programs, such as a sports panel, a television debate, a talk show interview, a news presentation.

Teacher preparation

- Videotape several television programs that demonstrate different voice and presentation styles. Students could help with this.
- Multiple copies of the Observations of Presenters sheet on page 87.

Activity

1. Prior to viewing the videotapes, ask students to list different TV shows that are live-to-air or involve a studio audience. Make a chart with three columns and record the program, the purpose, and the target audience.

2. Give out copies of the observation sheet. Explain that students are going to identify the way presenters purposefully modify their talk. Show the selected videotapes. Pause the video, when necessary, to guide the students' observations and to give them time to make notes.

3. After having completed the observation sheet, ask the students to consider:
   - the ways in which presenters adjust their voice and presentation style to match the audience and the subject matter; and
   - the relationship between the audience and the presenter.

4. Record student responses for future reference.

Extension/Variation

Have students record radio programs hosted by presenters. Have the class listen to extracts from these programs and record their observations on a sheet.

Student reflection
- Something I learned from observing the presenters' different use of voice and presentation style is . . .

Teacher reflection
- What level of support was needed with the observation sheet?
- Do students require further practice with this form of note taking?

Identifying and Using Good Questions

The purpose of this activity is to assist students in identifying questions for conducting an interview, including the techniques of using questions to probe for and clarify meaning.

Teacher preparation

A video of a popular interviewer engaged in face-to-face dialogue.

Activity

1. Ask students to name some of the interviewers they have seen or heard on the media and to recall anything they have noted about their technique; for example, the sort of questions they ask, the way they respond when the interviewee speaks, their facial expressions, their body movements, and gestures.

2. Watch a short interview given by a popular interviewer. Ask students to observe the interaction between the interviewer and the interviewee, and the way the interview is introduced and concluded.

3. Students share their observations.

4. Discuss the role of probing to clarify meaning and extend a response. Have students compile a list of probes that clarify meaning. For example: *Can you explain that a little further? Can you give me an example? What do you think is really important in this issue? How do you think this makes other people feel?*

5. Replay the video and identify the probes. Add to the list of probes.

Extension/Variation

Arrange for students to video a range of different interviewers. Have students critically listen and observe segments from the videos. Discuss how the audience and the topics covered influence the interviewers' use of language and their interaction with the interviewee.

Student reflection

- A question I will ask when I interview somebody is . . .
- A probe I would find useful to get information is . . .

Teacher reflection

- How observant are students of the techniques used by interviewers?
- Do I provide sufficient modelling of probes and clarifying questions or statements in class discussions?

QUESTIONS AND INTERVIEWS

Designing the Questions

The purpose of this activity is to assist students in designing interview questions that encourage people to talk more expansively.

Activity

1. Ask students to consider:
   - the type of questions they like being asked and those they don't like being asked; and
   - an occasion when they have thought carefully about the wording of a question they have asked.

2. Explain that interviewers need to plan their questions very carefully to get detailed responses from their interviewees. Questions with single-word responses should be avoided; for example, *Did you have a good weekend? Yes/No*. Have the students rephrase the question to encourage more detailed responses; for example, *Tell me about your weekend*. Practise several examples.

3. Divide students into pairs. Ask each pair to design five questions to ask their classmates about their own thoughts on fast food, homework, speed limits, sporting events, or questions related to a curriculum topic. Stress the importance of quality not quantity when designing questions.

4. Join pairs together. One person from each pair takes the role of interviewer and interviewee. The other pair acts as critical friends and report back about the use of the questions and the amount of detail in the responses. Swap roles.

5. Ask the students to share their most effective questions.

Extension/Variation

Tape-record or videotape students practising their questioning techniques.

Student reflection
- Something I need to remember when designing questions is . . .

Teacher reflection
- How competent are students at designing interview questions?
- How can the skills be applied to another key learning area so that students can consolidate their learning?

Talk-back Radio

FACT OR OPINION?

The purpose of this activity is to develop students' ability to listen for the main point and distinguish between fact and opinion. They will develop an awareness of the language used by broadcasters in response to callers.

Teacher preparation

Prepare some taped examples of several talk-back programs, or ask the class to tape their favorite talk-back segments.

Activity

1. Before listening to the taped programs, ask students to list times when radio talk-back occurs.

2. Brainstorm the reasons why:
   - radio stations have talk-back sessions; and
   - listeners use talk-back.

3. Students will need to listen to the tape several times. Play the taped examples once while students listen for the main ideas. List these on the board.

4. Play the tape again while students listen for examples of fact and opinion. List these on the board.

5. Ask students to listen for the words that indicate the broadcasters' approaches to the callers. For example, the words may indicate the following approaches: friendly/aggressive, condescending/supportive, dismissive.

6. Play the tape again while students note the type of language used by the broadcasters.

Extension/Variation

Facilitate a class discussion of the possible reasons for the different approaches taken by each broadcaster. Identify possible bias and suggest reasons for it.

Student reflection

- One new thing I learned about talk-back format is . . .

Teacher reflection

- To what extent are students able to use talk-back in another task? (See the Broadcasting Assessment Task on page 61.)

Student Reporters

The purpose of this activity is to give students regular practice in presenting short news reports to the class, using the skills that have been introduced in previous activities. Students in the audience are expected to demonstrate active listening by asking relevant questions or adding supportive comments after each report.

Activity

1. Invite students to recall recent interesting news items. List these.

2. Categorize the items under general headings, such as international news, entertainment, politics, and environment.

3. Explain that each day several students will be asked to report a relevant news item on a selected topic. Students will conclude their report with their own opinion of the issue or events that had taken place.

4. Students are to demonstrate active listening by asking questions that clarify their understanding or probe for meaning.

5. Discuss how audience participation can change the presentation.

6. Suggest that it is a useful strategy for students to anticipate questions they may be asked and the way they might respond. For example, the students may ask the reporter to explain the reasons for their opinion about the issue.

7. Revisit the learning about necessary information (who, why, when, what, where).

Extension/Variation

A weekly award could be established for the best presentation. Have the class determine the criteria on which the award will be judged, and vote for the recipient.

When the students become more confident, record their news stories on video or cassette for constructive review purposes.

Student reflection

● When I share a news item with the class I will remember to . . .

Teacher reflection

● What parts of students' news presentations require further practice?

● What do students' questions indicate about their engagement with the presentation?

Creating News Stories from Pictures

The purpose of this activity is to practise structuring news stories for different purposes and contexts. While the key focus questions must be covered and the main idea and supporting detail need to be explicit, the activity encourages students to create a story for a specific audience and context.

Teacher preparation

A collection of stimulus pictures taken from newspapers, magazines, and the Internet.

Activity

1. Show the class a picture that is likely to spark a strong response from the students.

2. Encourage students to imagine the story behind the picture.

3. Select a context and an audience for the story; for example, an assembly for lower primary students. Discuss how the audience will determine the delivery of the story. Jointly construct a story, providing the essential information, the main point, and the necessary supporting details.

4. Divide the class into groups and give each group a picture. Each group decides on an audience and the context in which the story will be heard; for example, a radio broadcast, television current affairs program, an assembly, or a local meeting. Set a time limit for each group to prepare an entertaining news story based on their picture, to share with the class.

5. Groups present their news stories.

6. Select friendly critics (see Glossary) to respond to each picture story.

Extension/Variation

Each group commissions a news story from another group. The news story must include a picture, the context, and the target audience.

Student reflection

● Our group was successful in . . .

Teacher reflection

● How effectively did the picture stories reflect the students' understanding of adapting reporting styles to audience and context?

Radio Programs

This task is designed to assess the understanding and skills introduced and practised in this unit. It is a group activity where individual students take different roles and responsibilities. Each group needs a minimum of five students of mixed abilities, who will need to take a variety of roles. Some roles are mandatory and some roles are negotiable. For example, the researcher is mandatory and the newsreader is negotiable.

The purpose of the task, the structure, assessment criteria, and methods should be made explicit to students at the beginning. The task should be given a specific timeframe and students should be assisted in planning and setting timelines and deadlines.

The number of segments per program should be adapted to suit the needs of the group. Some segments are mandatory, others negotiable. Lengthy segments, such as quizzes, should not be included.

Task description

Prepare and present a 10-minute radio broadcast to suit a particular:

● **context**—for example, the time of day, and location of the audience

● **audience**—for example, teenagers, mixed groups, elderly/retired, rural, urban

● **purpose**—for example, to entertain, inform, challenge, educate, or sell a product through advertisements

Structure

The broadcast may include several different segments, such as news items, interviews, talk-back, advertisements.

Assessment

Group and individual tasks will be student-assessed and teacher-assessed. Assessment criteria are listed on Radio Program Assessment—Mandatory Roles (see page 88) and Radio Program Assessment—Negotiable Roles (see page 89).

Production

All the group members are part of the production team. The team should elect a leader who runs the meetings.

The team will need to meet at regular intervals for members to report on their progress (planning and practice). As a team, the members share the following responsibilities:

● Plan the context, audience, and purpose of the program.

● Assign roles (students should have more than one role). All team members must do some broadcasting.

● Act as editorial group to decide on content and point of view so as to meet the needs of the audience and the purpose of the program.

● Develop a broad timeline for production and presentation.

The following lists individual responsibilities of specific team-member roles.

Mandatory roles and responsibilities	Negotiable roles and responsibilities
Director ● Develop running sheet of timeline and keep everyone on task and on time. ● Manage smooth transition from one segment to another. **Researcher** ● Assist the reporters with the background research. ● Prepare news reports. ● Find interesting people to interview. ● Develop challenging and relevant questions. **Co-hosts** **(two people to anchor the show)** ● Introduce specialist reporters. ● Run talk-back. ● Develop questions (with researchers) and conduct interviews. ● Manage smooth transition from one segment to another. **Technical and special effects** ● Develop and produce special effects as required. ● Manage the production of music as required. ● Ensure the production has appropriate volume and clarity.	**News readers** ● Work with researchers to write and edit the news. ● Read the news. **Writers and performers of advertisements** ● Make and perform advertisements. **Reporters** ● Work with researchers to develop stories. ● Report sports, weather, and current events.

Student Profile

Name: _____ Date: _____

This chart lists the skills that you have been practising as broadcasters. For each skill, place an X in the column that you think best describes your progress.

Assessment criteria	Occasionally	Usually	Consistently
I identify the main idea and supporting details when listening to reported information.			
I can identify different approaches when listening to reports of the same news items.			
I can distinguish between fact and opinion when listening to people talk.			
I adjust the way I talk to suit the audience.			
I use appropriate expressions and gestures when reporting information.			
I ask questions and respond when others present information.			
I can prepare a set of interview questions seeking information about a topic or issue.			
I use probes to extend a response.			
I use questions to clarify meaning.			
I am confident about using technology to support a spoken presentation.			

Something I do well when reporting information is: _____

_____

A goal I have set to improve my broadcasting techniques is: _____

_____

A skill I have learned or improved through participation in this unit is: _____

_____

Teacher's comments: _____

Let me Change Your Mind—

Many Points of View

At an early age children develop strategies that help them convince people of many things—giving them what they want; going where they want; even staying up until they want. As children grow older and become more proficient users of language they realize that words are an important tool to get people to accept ideas and opinions and even to change people's minds.

Persuasive talk can take different forms and can have different purposes. Examples of persuasive talk include: conversational talk to justify an action or proposed action; discussion to reveal different points of view; formal debates to express the affirmative and negative sides of a case; advertisements to sell or draw attention to products; and campaigns to promote change. Each context is dependent on different strategies and skills.

To participate successfully in debates students need to be critical thinkers who can confront an issue from different perspectives. Before attempting formal debating, there are some essential skills students need to develop. These include:

- expressing a point of view clearly and succinctly;
- presenting convincing arguments to support a point of view;
- using language appropriate to the situation;
- selecting vocabulary for impact;
- asking questions to clarify or challenge a position; and
- defending a point of view against an opposing one.

The activities in this unit focus on different purposes for persuasive talk, and on preparing students for formal debating.

PERSONAL OPINION/ POINT OF VIEW

Explaining My Position

The purpose of this activity is to give students the opportunity to think about and state their point of view. It is a short activity and best done before students begin to construct arguments to support their point of view.

Activity

1. Ask students to list the things about which they feel strongly; for example, a sporting team, a musical group, homework, a special interest, or an environmental issue. Make sure they keep the ideas general.

2. Provide some quiet time when students can think about why they feel strongly about a particular idea.

3. Explain that the purpose of the activity is to state a point of view together with one major supporting reason, not to explore the reasons. Model an example of the thinking from your own experience. Point of view: *I feel strongly that we should not have domestic pets.* One major supporting reason: *I believe in animal rights.* Keep the statement simple and do not provide any supporting argument.

4. Following your model, students explain their ideas to a partner. There is no opportunity for discussion at this stage.

5. Partners repeat each other's statements to the class.

6. Record statements that may be used in the activity, "What We Believe" (see page 67).

Extension/Variation

Students express a point of view and give two or three supporting reasons for their opinion. Have students focus on using persuasive words to convince their audience. For example: *I strongly believe . . .* ; *It is my firm opinion . . .* ; *I am convinced . . .* Record the best examples for future reference.

Student reflection

● It is important to support a point of view with reasons because . . .

● Some words or expressions that help me to put across my point of view persuasively are . . .

Teacher reflection

● To what degree were students able to express and support a point of view?

● What understanding did students demonstrate of using persuasive language to make their opinions heard?

Presenting and Contesting Points of View

The purpose of this activity is to introduce students to the use of appropriate language when presenting and challenging a point of view.

Activity

1. Write a contestable statement, such as "Homework is really important."
2. Explain the purpose of the activity.
3. Present the rules (see below).
4. Explain that students can change their minds and challenge opinions.
5. Ask students for opinions that challenge or support the statement.

Rules

- Students must use the stems provided.
- All ideas should be relevant.
- Supporting evidence for opinions can be offered.
- No ideas can be repeated.
- No negative body language.

Stems

- It is reasonable to say that . . .
- That idea is incorrect because . . .
- If you examine the evidence given by . . . you can see that . . .
- It is commonly accepted that . . .
- The idea put forward by . . . does not take this idea into account . . .
- There is another way of looking at this . . .

Extension/Variation

Assign students to play the role of the "devil's advocate" by putting forward alternative positions. Inform students it is not necessary that they believe the view put forward.

Student reflection

- Times when I need to challenge another person's point of view include . . .
- I feel a little more/a lot more confident about challenging a point of view because . . .

Teacher reflection

- Do students require further opportunities for the development of this skill?
- How could this skill be implemented across key learning areas?

"What We Believe"— Using Supportive Arguments

The purpose of this activity is to develop students' understanding that their position on an issue is more likely to be accepted if they can provide convincing, supportive arguments. Statements developed by students in "Explaining My Position" can be used (see page 65).

Activity

1. Choose one statement about which there is general consensus. List on the board all the arguments students suggest that support the position. For example, Too much homework is unfair.

2. Have students rank their arguments and decide on the three most convincing points.

3. Divide the class into groups. Have each group choose an issue and repeat the process demonstrated, explaining that the group is to use the five strongest points to support its position. Explain that the audience will be assessing the consistency and relevancy of the arguments.

4. Tell the class to listen critically as each group presents an argument, preparing to ask for clarification if a point is not clear, and to challenge any point that is not consistent with the group's position. Remind students of appropriate ways to challenge (see Unit 1).

5. Facilitate a discussion on the importance of presenting arguments that are consistent and relevant when expressing a position on an issue.

Extension/Variation

Set aside a lunch time for "soapbox presentations" in the schoolyard. Set a strict timeframe (one to two minutes) for presentations on issues about which students feel passionately. Awards could be given for different categories, such as the presentation that best achieved the most audience support, and the most entertaining presentation.

Student reflection

- An important point to remember when presenting a position is . . .
- The students who were the most convincing held the audience's attention by . . .

Teacher reflection

- How convincing were students in presenting their positions?
- What links can be made with written expression to reinforce the skills students are developing?

Justifying an Action

The purpose of this activity is to develop students' ability to justify an action or a request, giving well-considered reasons.

Activity

1. Have students recall situations when they have had to justify an action or a proposed action; for example, explaining to a teacher why they are late for class, or seeking permission from a parent to go out with friends.

2. Following the example below, brainstorm other situational contexts when students may need to justify their action or proposed action. Record these on cards.

Situation	Person who must be convinced
You want to go skateboarding in the city with friends.	Your mother, who thinks the city is off limits unless there is an adult accompanying you.

3. Give partners a scenario to role-play. Ask students to consider how both the situation and the person who has to be convinced will influence the style of language used and the reasoning given. Explain that arguments must be challenged if they do not sound convincing.

4. Choose several of the role plays for presentation to the whole class.

5. Discuss in what ways the social and situational contexts influenced the use of language.

Extension/Variation

Students practise convincing others of an action or a proposed action, in one-minute timeslots.

Student reflection

- I can be more convincing when I remember to . . .
- What things influence the language I use to justify an action or a request?

Teacher reflection

- How purposefully were students able to justify their use of language to accommodate the social and situational contexts?

Arguments For and Against

The purpose of this activity is to give students practice in thinking about two sides of an argument. It provides a useful strategy for predicting likely questions when preparing a talk for an audience.

Activity

1. Explain to the class that some issues are contentious and that people have divided opinions. For example, some people support Canada becoming part of the United States, while others would prefer Canada to remain a country on its own. Ask students to think of issues at school where opinion is divided. List their suggestions on the board. Other issues may be compulsory school uniforms, use of animals in scientific testing.

2. Draw two columns on the board labelled For and Against. Choose an issue and have students brainstorm the arguments for and against, recording these in the appropriate columns (see sample below). If one side has a noticeably uneven number of arguments, encourage students to try to correct the imbalance.

3. Divide the class into groups. Each group divides a sheet of paper into two columns labelled

Reasons for compulsory school uniform	Reasons against compulsory school uniform
• Saves time • The public gets to know the school	• It stops you being an individual • Uniforms are unfashionable

For and Against. They choose an issue and spend four minutes brainstorming arguments for both columns.

4. Have the groups share their arguments. The audience may seek clarification or challenge any arguments seen to be inconsistent or irrelevant.

5. Discuss how strong opinions may prevent a person from seeing the other side of an argument. Introduce the term "bias" and have students think of examples of one-sidedness, intolerance, or prejudice, which are all forms of bias.

6. Have students reflect on strategies they used to balance their views.

Extension/Variation

Encourage students to look for examples of bias in the media. Make a collection of articles that present only one point of view, or that report behaviour that is intolerant or prejudiced.

Student reflection

• I think it would be useful to use this strategy when . . .

• Something I learned about developing an arguments is . . .

Teacher reflection

• What application could this technique have in other key learning areas?

• What other situations exist for exploring the concept of biased opinions (such as strong points presented in texts)?

The Panel

The purpose of this activity is to give students the opportunity to consider an issue from different perspectives. It involves students representing community interest groups participating in a panel discussion. The audience is encouraged to question or challenge the arguments presented by the panel.

Activity

1. Present the scenario of the amalgamation of two local schools. Ask the students to imagine the response of different members of the community, such as parents, teachers, students. Discuss.

2. Divide the students into six groups. Explain that the class is going to have a panel discussion about the government giving permission to a timber company to cut down local trees for woodchipping in a national park.

3. Have each group consider the perspective of one of the following people:
   - the manager of the timber company
   - a representative of the foreign company who buys the wood chips
   - a logger employed by the timber company
   - a local resident
   - a representative of an environment group
   - the Minister for the Environment.

4. Encourage students to do some research about logging issues. Have each group choose one person as its representative on the panel. The group prepares the case. The group members may take other roles and be called upon by the group's panel representative to provide information during the discussion. Remind the panel representatives for each group of the importance of summarizing the main point/points at the end of their presentations.

5. After each group's panel representative has presented their case, ask for questions or challenges from the audience. Group members can support their panel representative to respond to questions.

6. Involve the whole class in a discussion of:
   - how strong opinions (bias) can stop a person from seeing another point of view; and
   - whether any students changed their thinking about the issue after hearing different perspectives.

Extension/Variation

Organize panel discussion on other issues; for example, homelessness, whaling, banning smoking in restaurants, the use of pesticides. Invite students to prepare a list of topics that might be of interest for class discussion. Allow time for independent research.

Student reflection

- I think it is important to consider all sides of an issue because . . .
- People have different perspectives on an issue because . . .

Teacher reflection

- How effective were the speakers in arguing from their perspective, summarizing the main points, and responding to questions?

CHALLENGING A POINT OF VIEW

When to Disagree

The purpose of this activity is to explore the nature of a proposed argument, and to develop strategies to assist students in identifying why a particular point of view can be challenged.

Teacher preparation

Explain that there are particular aspects which students can identify as contestable in arguments. Provide the students with the following list.

- The argument contained incorrect information (for example, statistics).
- The argument was based on an incorrect assumption.
- The argument was not relevant to the topic.
- The argument was trivial and of minor importance.
- The evidence was contradictory to the main point of the argument.
- The evidence was repetitive, that is, one point was made several times.

Activity

1. Work with students to define "argument."
2. Practise using the ideas in the list above with the class seated in pairs facing each other. One student makes a statement supported by an argument and the student opposite has to disagree, using one of the points from the list. Encourage students to make amusing or outlandish claims so that opportunities to contest arguments occur; for example, school holiday should be limited to two weeks a year; the price of gasoline should be doubled to protect the environment.
3. Explain that students may only refer to the argument and not to the person who said it; for example, "That argument contained incorrect statistics." rather than "John's idea contained incorrect statistics."
4. Conclude with the student reflection (see below).

Extension/Variation

- Look for examples in the media where the points in the list are used to challenge an argument.
- Use stems from the list for challenging arguments when playing devil's advocate.

Student reflection

- Points of view are not acceptable when . . .
- The points of view that were easiest to challenge were . . .

Teacher reflection

- To what degree were students able to successfully identify why a particular point needed to be challenged?
- A difficulty that some students experienced with this activity was . . .

What Do I Assume?

CHALLENGING A POINT OF VIEW

Students are better able to analyze their own opinions and those of others if they can identify the assumptions on which the opinions are based. The purpose of this activity is to identify assumptions. It may generate a lot of discussion. Students may have to be reminded of the purpose.

Activity

1. Present a simple, familiar scenario; for example: The principal comes into the classroom looking very serious.

2. Ask the students for assumptions they might make about the situation; for example, the students have done something wrong, someone is hurt, the teacher is in trouble, the principal is tired. List the assumptions on the board and complete a chart similar to the sample below.

3. Extend the chart adding further assumptions, or develop another scenario.

Scenario	Assumption	Reason	Reasonable/ Unreasonable assumption
The principal comes into the class looking very serious	• The class is in trouble • Someone is hurt	• The class is often in trouble	• Reasonable
The teacher buys the class chocolate covered peanuts	• No one is allergic to peanuts • All students deserve an equal treat	• The teacher has never taught a student who is allergic to peanuts	• Unreasonable

4. Ask students to suggest occasions when they think it could be useful to identify underlying assumptions, such as when viewing advertisements or considering an umpire's decision.

Extension/Variation

Students review a media broadcast, such as a talk show or a current affairs program to identify some of the underlying assumptions.

Student reflection

• An assumption is . . .
• Being able to identify assumptions will help me to . . .
• Something I find challenging about identifying assumptions is . . .

Teacher reflection

• How challenging did students find this activity? In what ways might I approach this activity differently next time?
• What other opportunities could I provide for students to practise identifying assumptions?

PERSUASIVE TALK

Analyzing Advertisements

The purpose of this activity is to familiarize students with how advertisements use language to persuade or convince people about the product they are promoting.

Activity

1. Invite students to volunteer their favorite advertisements and explain why they find them appealing. List responses on the board.

2. Ask students to consider how language is used in advertisements to promote products or services.

3. Display the chart of language strategies used in advertisements (see Advertising Technique Chart on page 90). Discuss the meaning of each one and how these strategies are designed to influence people's thinking. Ask students to suggest advertisements that they think fit the first two strategies in the list.

4. Divide the students into groups and ask them to complete the chart.

5. Share the groups' findings. Discuss the language strategies they find the most powerful. Have students suggest other language strategies they identify with advertisements.

Extension/Variation

- Students record a range of advertisements and present them to the class to analyze.

- Have students identify how sound enhances advertisements. Consider the use of background music, songs, tone and pitch of people's voices, and special effects.

Student reflection

- The techniques I frequently hear used in advertisements are . . .

- The techniques I find the most powerful are . . .

Teacher reflection

- Which techniques did students find easy/difficult to identify?

- To what extent are students able to critically analyze the techniques introduced?

DEBATING

Getting the Facts

The purpose of this activity is to implement the skills developed in this unit and to introduce debating.

Activity

1. Ask students if they have ever watched or participated in a debate and discuss the purpose of debating.

2. Explain the difference between discussion and debate:
   - In a discussion the participants explore a problem or issue and search for an answer.
   - In a debate, one assumes they have the right answer and sets out to prove their answer is correct. Each debater also tries to persuade the listener to agree with his or her opinion.

3. Explain the format of a debate. It is recommended that only one debate be presented in one day and a time limit be set for each speaker (30 seconds to one minute or longer if the students are advanced).

3. Arrange students in groups of eight. Four members of the group will be the team for the issue assigned and four will be the team against (opposition). Each group of eight will have a different issue to debate. Issues should be challenging and thought provoking; for example, homeless people should not be allowed in our cities or all sports athletes should a have a cap on their salary which would not exceed $80 000.

4. Allow each team time to research their topic and develop evidence to support their opinion. Evidence can be in the form of a fact, example, statistic, quotation, or source.

5. Teams must prioritize the information and select four main points to use in their debate that will prove their point of view. Each team member will present one of the four points.

6. Each team must also consider which of their points the opposition may rebut or refute in order to disprove what they say and prepare a rebuttal of their own.

7. When all of the information is collected and organized, the group must decide who will make what point and in what order. Should the strongest speaker go first or last? Should the strongest point be presented first or last? (These are presentation strategies that will effect the persuasion of the listeners.)

8. Conclude with the student reflection.

Extension/Variation

- Hold a debate using the blackline masters Structure of a Debate and Voting Criteria for a Debate (see pages 91 and 92).

Student reflection

- The research proved to me that . . .
- While in the debate, I am concerned that . . .

Teacher reflection

- Did the students work together as a team? How could I further facilitate their cooperation?
- How could I assist students in their preparation to speak?

Student Profile

Name: _____   Date: _____

This chart lists the skills that you have been practising in developing and presenting your point of view. For each skill, place an X in the column that you think best describes your progress.

Assessment criteria	Occasionally	Usually	Consistently
I am able to clearly state an opinion or point of view.			
I construct arguments that support my opinions.			
I can argue a case from different perspectives.			
I can identify strategies used by speakers to influence an audience.			
I can challenge arguments that are inconsistent or unclear.			
I respond to ideas rather than to people.			
I disagree politely.			
I identify assumptions that underlie opinions.			
I can discuss whether an assumption is reasonable.			
I can identify the emotive techniques used in advertisements.			
I can debate with clarity and confidence.			

My greatest strength when using persuasive talk is: _____

_____

Something I still find challenging: _____

_____

Goals I have set myself: _____

_____

Teacher's comment: _____

Resource Bank

This section contains an overview for each unit and photocopiable resources for students and teachers. The student blackline masters can be used as is, and then adapted by teachers for further speaking and listening projects.

- Unit at a Glance
- Teacher Checklist for Establishing a Collaborative Classroom
- Checklist for Effective Communication
- Group Assessment Sheet
- Framework of Questions for Planning a Task
- Student–Student Interaction
- Let Me Tell You a Story Assessment Sheet
- Observations of Presenters
- Radio Program Assessment—Mandatory Roles
- Radio Program Assessment—Negotiable Roles
- Advertising Technique Chart
- Structure of a Debate
- Voting Criteria for a Debate

Unit 1: At a Glance

Tuning In—Speakers and Listeners

Focus	Activity	Skill (The student will...)
Active Listening	Hearing Ears What Was the Message? Hearing Between the Lines	• Listen to remember • Listen for detail • Listen for implied meaning
Informative Listening	Follow Me Finding the Right Solution I Say You Said Experts	• Follow and give instructions • Brainstorm and prioritize information • State and summarize an opinion • Summarize and report information
Engaging in dialogue—Student Interaction	Mapping Our Talk Sharing Talk-time Exploring Reasons Step by Step	• Identify and re-establish communication patterns • Become aware of equal opportunity to speak • Ask questions to clarify opinions • Interact with other people's ideas
Collaborating	Role Switch This Is Not a Conversation! Consensus	• Participate actively in a group with specified roles • Engage in a discussion • Collaborate to reach a consensus
Developing Questioning Strategies	Asking in Class Seek and Find	• Practise strategies for asking questions in class • Practise strategies for asking questions in public places
Clarifying Meaning	Oh, No! What's All That Stuff?	• Express meaning through voice and body language • Discuss the meaning of words in context

Unit 2: At a Glance

Tell Me the Story—Stories and Storytellers

Focus	Activity	Skill (The student will...)
Narrative Frameworks	Telling Your Own Fairy Stories Modern Versions of Fairy Stories Personal Stories	● Collaboratively create and present a fairy story ● Explore linguistic structures and features of a traditional narrative ● Recount personal stories
Strategies for Engaging the Audience	Readers' Theatre The Town Crier Chairs in Pairs Shorts (30-second or one-minute presentations) Using a Storyboard Let Me Tell You a Story Telling the Poem	● Practise audience involvement strategies ● Practise exaggeration strategies ● Practise persuasion strategies ● Select and present presentation strategies ● Create and use visual cues for presentation ● Rehearse a written piece for presentation ● Present as entertainment

Unit 3: At a Glance

So What's New—Broadcasters

Focus	Activity	Skill (The student will...)
Broadcasting—Structural Organization	Can You Identify? Viewing the News Same News Item, Different Story	• Listen for main ideas and supporting details • Identify news styles • Compare content of news services
Awareness of Context, Audience, and Purpose	Speaking the Part	• Compare styles of television presenters
Questions and Interviews	Identifying and Using Good Questions Designing the Questions	• Identify good interview questions • Design probing interview questions
Fact or Opinion?	Talk-back Radio	• Distinguish between fact and opinion
Using the Skills	Student Reporters Creating News Stories From Pictures	• Present news reports and question reporters • Create and present fictional news stories
Broadcasting Assessment Task	Radio Programs?	• Assume a role and prepare a broadcast for presentation

Unit 4: At a Glance

Let Me Change Your Mind—Many Points of View

Focus	Activity	Skill (The student will...)
Personal Opinion/Point of View	Explaining My Position Presenting and Contesting Points of View "What We Believe"—Using Supportive Arguments Justifying an Action	• Express a personal point of view • Explore appropriate language for challenging a point of view • Explore convincing and supportive arguments • Explore ways to justify an action or a request
Many Sides to the Argument	Arguments For and Against The Panel	• Explore two sides of an argument and predict questions for the other side • Participate in a panel discussion representing an issue
Strategies for Challenging a Point of View or an Opinion	When to Disagree What Do I Assume?	• Explore the meaning of argument and use contesting points of view • Explore and identify assumptions that lead to misguided opinions
Persuasive Talk	Analyzing Advertisements	• Explore and identify strategies used in persuasive advertising
Debating	Getting The Facts	• Research and develop a debate

Teacher Checklist for Establishing a Collaborative Classroom

The following checklist outlines some key points that should assist teachers in providing a supportive environment that encourages students to become active, independent learners. The points covered are a source for guiding teachers' reflection on their discussion techniques.

- Establish a relaxed and nurturing atmosphere.

- Provide time for students to organize their thoughts.

- Acknowledge students' responses without giving effusive praise.

- Encourage student–student dialogue by vacating the floor and becoming a participant in the discussion (see Glossary).

- Ask open-ended questions that do not have predetermined answers.

- Focus on fewer, carefully chosen questions and sustain these with probes.

- Model questions to clarify meaning and to seek elaboration of responses.

- Encourage students to question one another.

- Use alternatives to questions, such as comments, to foster talk.

- Turn student responses back to the group for further comment.

- Avoid taking over the students' thinking by reformulating their responses with additional ideas.

- Check that summaries are an accurate representation of the class's thinking.

- Listen actively and challenge students' thinking.

- Discourage repetitious anecdotes and retelling of a storyline.

- Model thinking aloud.

- Encourage students' exploration of reasoning.

Checklist for Effective Communication

When speaking I should remember to:

- adjust my talk to suit the purpose of the task and the audience
- make eye contact with the person/people to whom I am speaking
- control the expression and volume of my voice
- talk on the point and avoid becoming side-tracked
- check the feedback from the audience and adjust my talk if necessary
- respond thoughtfully to questions.

When listening I should remember to:

- give my full attention to the person who is speaking
- wait until the speaker has finished before replying
- reply considerately when someone speaks to me
- respect differences of opinions
- ask questions to clarify meaning or seek additional information.

As a responsible group member I should remember to:

- contribute my ideas, experiences, and opinions
- encourage everyone to take part
- consider situations from other points of view
- help the group to reach consensus
- monitor my interaction and the group interaction.

Helpful leads to support interaction:

- Can you explain that a little more fully?
- How are you using the word . . .?
- Is there a difference between . . . and . . .?
- Are you saying that . . .?
- Could you give us an example . . .?

Ways to support an idea or a point of view:

- I agree with . . .
- I would like to add to that idea . . .
- In support of what you said . . .
- Another idea that supports your point of view . . .

Courteous ways to disagree:

- That's an interesting idea, but I can see a different one.
- I would like to give another point of view.
- What are your reasons for saying that?

Group Assessment Sheet

Place a cross on the continuum 1–10 to indicate your group's assessment for each statement.

Everybody had a turn.

We listened actively.

Only one person spoke at a time.

We used each other's ideas.

We discussed different points of view.

We asked for clarification.

We encouraged quieter members.

We kept on the topic.

We made eye contact.

We used time efficiently.

We negotiated fairly.

We reached consensus.

One way in which our group worked successfully: _____

_____

_____

Goals we want to achieve when next we work together: _____

_____

_____

_____

_____

Framework of Questions for Planning a Task

Questions about intention

- What do I want to do?
- How important is it?

Questions about place

- Where do I want to do it? (school, home, library, IT area, etc.)
- Where will I start?

Questions about timing

- When is it due?
- When will I start each section?
- How long will each section take?
- When will each section be finished?
- How long will the whole task take?
- When will I hand it to the teacher?

Questions about resources

- What resources do I need?

Questions about people

- Who will help?
- What will they help with?
- How will I negotiate the help?

Student–Student Interaction

Recorder: _____

Two-way interaction

One-way interaction

Let Me Tell You a Story
Assessment Sheet

Name: _____ Date: _____

Title of myth, legend, or fable: _____

Complete the following so that the teacher and your critical friend can assess your work.

● Part of the narrative emphasised (for example, sequence of events)

_____

_____

● How do you want the audience to feel? (for example, nervous, excited, tense)

_____

_____

● How will you achieve this? (for example, by using lots of pauses)

_____

_____

● Other strategies for engaging the audience (for example, students participating at some points):

_____

_____

● Other aspects of my story telling I would like to be assessed on (for example, an unusual introduction)

_____

_____

Signed: _____   Signed: _____

(presenter) _____   (critical friend) _____

Observations of Presenters

	Show 1	Show 2	Show 3
Program and presenter			
Purpose of the show			
Target audience			
Voice: ● pitch of talk ● pace of talk ● tone of talk			
Talk style: ● emphasis on facts or opinions ● use of proper English ● colloquialisms, abbreviations and slang ● expression of personal feelings and emotions			
Body language: ● stance, hand gestures ● facial expression, body movements ● dress style			

Radio Program Assessment—
Mandatory Roles

Name: _____ Date: _____

Group members: _____

Assessment criteria	Occasionally	Usually	Consistently
Production team Everyone felt comfortable in the group. Talents were used and recognized. Everyone contributed well. The group was able to make decisions and develop a sensible timeline. The group was able to overcome difficulties.			
Director I kept good records of what was to happen. I kept to the timeline. My suggestions were listened to. I kept the broadcast flowing freely.			
Researcher My information was interesting and addressed who, what, when, where, and why. My information was relevant. The interview added extra interest. The questions drew out interesting responses.			
Co-hosts The program ran smoothly. Our voices were lively and varied. We distinguished between fact and opinion in talk-back. We treated callers with respect. We encouraged interviewers to explore and explain ideas. We recognized the team who helped pull the show together.			
Technical and special effects Programs could be heard clearly. Technical effects were stimulating. Technical effects supported the presentations.			

Radio Program Assessment— Negotiable Roles

Name: _____ Date: _____

Group members: _____

Assessment criteria	Occasionally	Usually	Consistently
News readers The news stories contained facts of who, what, when, where, and why. Fact and opinion were presented separately. News items were clearly explained.			
Writers and performers of advertisements Advertisements caught the attention of the audience. Advertisements were short and varied. Both fact and opinion were used. Emotive language was used.			
Reporters Our reports contained basic information of who, where, when, what, and why. The information was relevant. Opinions were recognized. Reports were expressed clearly.			

Advertising Technique Chart

Name: _____ Date: _____

Group members: _____

The language of advertising	Radio or television advertisement
1. Repetition: certain words repeated for impact.	
2. Play on words: emphasis on words such as **free, bargain, reduced price, cheap**.	
3. Words that stress urgency: **do not delay, special offer** for a **limited time** only.	
4. Exaggeration: **best** test results, **greenest** lawn, **most popular** author, dogs' **favorite** food.	
5. Family welfare: being urged to protect the interests and well-being of your family.	
6. Transfer of experience: **use this product, take this action** and **this could be you**.	
7. Be patriotic: support your country	
8. Innuendo: inferring that no other product or service is as good.	
9. Use of humor: appealing to people's desire to be entertained.	
10. Oversimplifying: **all it takes to achieve this result is . . .**	

Adapted from Dalton (1985).

Structure of a Debate

1. There are two sides, or two teams that debate an issue—for and against. Both teams must prepare what they will say using research and evidence. There will be four people on a team. Each member of each team will have an opportunity to speak.

2. The team that opens has the responsibility of establishing the foundation of the debate. Member one of team one will speak first, then member two, then three, and lastly four. Then team two will begin to speak. Member one of team two will speak and state the first point, but will also refute (or rebut) something that was said by a member of the other team. Similarly, when member two speaks, they will make their point and also refute something that was said by team one, and so on. When all of team two has spoken, team one has an opportunity to rebut what team two said. Once team one has refuted team two's comments, the debate is over.

3. If time allows, the audience may ask questions of any team member regarding clarify on a point. Finally, the audience votes on which team they feel 'won' the debate. This vote is based on preparation, evidence presented, and presentation qualities such as, poise, passion, energy and clarity. (List the basis of voting on a chart). Throughout the debate the teacher may act as the moderator to keep the debate moving along.

Voting Criteria for a Debate

Consider the following points before casting your vote.

Did the speaker . . .	Yes	Somewhat	No
look prepared			
clearly state their opinion			
appear poised and confident			
enunciate their words and use proper sentences			
use passion and energy to excite the audience			
refute the opposing teams' points			

Glossary

Aural memory is memory based on what was heard. "Aural" relates to hearing or listening.

Direct speech is when the words actually spoken are presented in writing, for example: *Harry said, "Don't forget to bring the soccer ball to the park."* This is the most dramatic way to present speech because it is written directly as it was said.

Fluency refers to talk which flows smoothly and easily.

Friendly critic in the classroom is a supportive classmate who understands what the student is trying to do, and is prepared to constructively suggest improvements without hurting the student's feelings.

Indirect speech is when the words spoken are reported by the writer, for example: *Harry told me not to forget to bring the soccer ball to the park*. The impact of the original words is partially lost.

Intonation is associated with the changes in pitch when people talk. There are noticeable differences in the pitch of people's voices at the beginning and the ending of a story or when making a point.

Pace refers to the speed of delivering talk. It can be very even or it can vary by speeding up or slowing down talk.

Pausing is making a temporary stop before a word or a passage when talking in order to capture the audience's attention.

Pitch refers to the tone of the voice and is often associated with certain feelings and emotions. When people are excited, the pitch of their voice rises. When people are upset, the pitch of their voice is often lower.

PMI is a problem-solving strategy devised by Edward de Bono. It involves listing all the positive or plus (**P**) and negative or minus (**M**) aspects associated with a situation, in addition to ideas which are neither positive or negative but may be categorized as interesting (**I**) to consider.

Stress refers to the emphasis placed on a word or part of a word to highlight it or make it stand out in a passage.

Vacating the floor is a term used by Christine Perrott (1988) which refers to teachers' preparedness to step back from classroom discussion, allowing students to interact with one another. It does not mean relinquishing control, but reminds teachers of the need to avoid dominating the talk, and to become a participant in the discussion with the students.

Volume relates to changes in the loudness or softness of talk. It is different from stress in that stress can be varied without altering the volume.

Note: Definitions relating to voice are adapted from *Talking to Learn* (Jones, 1996).

Selected Bibliography

Baker, Deirdre and Ken Setterington. *A Guide to Canadian Children's Books*. Toronto, ON: McClelland & Stewart, 2003.

Barnes, Douglas. *Communication to Curriculum*. Portsmouth, NH: Boynton/Cook, 1995.

Barton, Bob. *Telling Stories Your Way*. Markham, ON: Pembroke Publishers, 2000.

Booth, David and Almuth Bartl. *Everybody Wins*. Markham, ON: Pembroke Publishers, 2000.

Booth, David and Bob Barton. *Story Works*. Markham, ON: Pembroke Publishers, 2000.

Booth, David and Larry Swartz. *Literacy Techniques for Building Successful Readers and Writers*, 2nd ed. Markham, ON: Pembroke Publishers, 2004.

Booth, David. *Stories to Read Aloud*. Markham, ON: Pembroke Publishers, 1992.

Bruner, J. *The Culture of Education*. Cambridge: Harvard University Press, 1996.

Buis, Kellie. *Writing Every Day*. Markham, ON: Pembroke Publishers, 2004.

Burke, Jim. *Tools for Thought*. Portsmouth, NH: Heinemann, 2002.

Carreiro, P. *Tales of Thinking: Multiple Intelligences in the Classroom*. Portland, ME: Stenhouse Publishers, 1998.

Chambers, Aidan. *Tell Me: Children, Reading, and Talk*. Portland, ME: Stenhouse Publishers, 1996.

Dalton, J. *Adventures in Thinking: Creative Thinking and Cooperative Talk in Small Groups*. Melbourne: Nelson, 1985.

Daniels, Harvey. *Literature Circles*, 2nd ed. Portland, ME: Stenhouse Publishers, 2001.

Davies, A. et al. *Together Is Better: Collaborative Assessment, Evaluation and Reporting*. Winnipeg: Peguis, 1992.

De Bono, E. *CoRT Thinking Program Guide*. London: Macmillam/McGraw-Hill, 1991.

Dorn, Linda J. and Carla Soffos. *Shaping Literate Minds*. Portland, ME: Stenhouse Publishers, 2001.

Dunn, Sonja. *All Together Now*. Markham, ON: Pembroke Publishers, 2000.

Edwards, A. and D. Westgate. *Investigating Classroom Talk*. London: The Falmer Press, 1994.

Elkin, Judith (ed.) *The Puffin Twentieth Century Collection of Stories*. London: Puffin, 1999.

Foster, Graham. *Language Arts Idea Bank*. Markham, ON: Pembroke Publishers, 2003.

Fox, Mem. *Teaching Drama to Young Children*. Portsmouth, NH: Heinemann, 1990.

French, Fiona. *Snow White in New York*. Oxford: Oxford University Press, 1986.

Gibbons, Pauline. *Scaffolding Language, Scaffolding Learning*. Portsmouth, NH: Heinemann, 2002.

Golub, Jeffrey N. *Making Learning Happen*. Portsmouth, NH: Boynton/Cook, 2000.

Greenwood Bob and Barbara Greenwood. *Speak Up! Speak Out!* Markham, ON: Pembroke Publishers, 1994.

Hahn, Mary Lee. *Reconsidering Read-Aloud*. Portland, ME: Stenhouse Publishers, 2002.

Jones, P. (ed.) *Talking to Learn*. Newtown, NSW: Primary English Teaching Association, 1996.

Kaufman, Douglas. *Conferences and Conversations*. Portsmouth, NH: Heinemann, 2000.

Krogness, Mary Mercer. *Just Teach Me, Mrs. K.* Portsmouth, NH: Heinemann, 1994.

Miyata, Cathy. *Speaking Rules!* Markham, ON: Pembroke Publishers, 2001.

Morgan, Norah and Juliana Saxton. *Asking Better Questions*. Markham, ON: Pembroke Publishers, 1991.

O'Keefe, Virginia. *Developing Critical Thinking: The Speaking/Listening Connection*. Portsmouth, NH: Boynton/Cook, 1999.

Opitz, Michael F. and Timothy V. Rasinski. *Good-bye Round Robin*. Portsmouth, NH: Heinemann, 2004.

Pennac, Daniel. *Better Than Life*. Markham, ON: Pembroke Publishers/Portland, ME: Stenhouse Publishers, 1999.

Pepper, Dennis (ed.) *The Oxford Book of Supernatural Stories*. Oxford: Oxford University Press, 1996.

Perrott, C. *Classroom Talk and Classroom Learning: Guidelines for Education*. Sydney: HBJ Publishers, 1988.

Pierce, K. and C. Gilles. *Cycles of Meaning: Exploring the Potential of Talk in Learning Communities*. Portsmouth, NH: Heinemann, 1993.

Rubright, Lynn. *Beyond the Beanstalk*. Portsmouth, NH: Heinemann, 1996.

Santi, M. 'Philosophising and learning to think: Some proposals for a qualitative evaluation in thinking,' *The Journal of Philosophy for Children*, vol. 10, no. 3, pp. 16–22, 1993.

Staab, Clarie. *Oral Language for Today's Classroom*. Toronto: Pippin, 2001.

Styles, Donna. *Class Meetings*. Markham, ON: Pembroke Publishers, 2001.

Swartz, Larry. *The New Drama Themes*, 3rd ed. Markham, ON: Pembroke Publishers, 2002.

Tarlington, Carole and Patrick Verriour. *Role Drama*. Markham, ON: Pembroke Publishers, 1991.

Trelease, Jim. *The Read-aloud Handbook*, 5th ed. New York, NY: Penguin, 2001.

Watts, Irene. *Making Stories*. Markham, ON: Pembroke Publishers, 1992.

Index

Active listening, 13–15, 59
  Hearing between the lines, 15
  Hearing ears, 13
  What was the message?, 14
Advertising technique chart, 73, 90
Anecdotes, 38, 43, 81
Argument, 5, 71
Assessment and evaluation, 10–11
At a Glance
  Unit 1, 77
  Unit 2, 78
  Unit 3, 79
  Unit 4, 80
Audience involvement, 40
Aural memory, 13
Awareness of context, audience, and purpose, 55
  Speaking the part, 55

Bias, 69, 70
Body language, 42, 66, 87
Brainstorming, 12, 14, 17, 20, 25, 28, 32, 35, 38, 43, 58, 68, 69
Broadcasting assessment task, 58, 61–62
  Radio programs, 61–62
Broadcasting—Structural organization, 50–54
  Can you identify?, 50–51
  Same news item, different story, 54
  Viewing the news, 52–53

Challenging a point of view, 71–72
  What do I assume?, 72
  When to disagree, 71
Checklist for effective communication, 11, 82
Clarifying meaning, 31–32, 56
  Oh, no!, 31
  What's all that stuff?, 32
Clarity, 9

Collaborating, 25–28
  Consensus, 28
  Role switch, 25
  This is not a conversation!, 26–27
Collaboration, 10, 25–27
Collaborative inquiry, 5, 7, 8, 9, 10
Communication patterns, 20
Communication skills, 5, 7, 10, 12
Conceptual understanding, 9
Conducting an interview, 56
Consensus, 28, 54, 67, 83
Consistency, 9
Constructing meaning, 31
Constructivism, 5, 7
Conversation, 26
Critical friend, 45, 46, 57, 86

Debating, 74, 91, 92
  Formal, 64
  Getting the facts, 74
  Structure, 74, 91
  Voting criteria, 74, 92
Designer, 25
Developing questioning strategies, 29–30
  Asking in class, 29
  Seek and find, 30
Direct speech, 40
Discussion, 5, 11, 26, 27, 32, 72, 74, 81
Discussion skills, 8–9
Diversity, 9

Encourager, 25
Engaging in dialogue, 20–24
  Exploring reasons, 23
  Mapping our talk, 20
  Sharing talk-time, 22
  Step by step, 24
Engaging the audience, 40–47
Evidence, 9
Exploratory talk, 8
Explore ideas, 26

Facial expression, 31, 42, 56
Facilitator, 9, 10, 27
Fact or opinion?, 58
  Talk-back radio, 58
Flexibility, 9
Formal debating, 64
Framework of questions for planning a task, 84
Friendly critic, 60

Getting the facts, 74
Giving detailed directions, 16
Group assessment sheet, 11, 20, 36, 40, 83

Identifying assumptions, 72
Implied meaning, 5, 15
Indirect speech, 40
Informative listening, 16–19
  Experts, 19
  Finding the right situation, 17
  Follow me, 16
  I say you said, 18
Insight, 5
Interact with others' ideas, 26
Interaction patterns, 20, 21, 24
Intervention, 10
Intonation, 40, 41

Justification, 5

Leader, 25
Let me tell you a story assessment sheet, 45, 86
Listening skills, 7, 9, 10, 13, 14, 16, 18
Listening to direction, 16

Many sides to the argument, 69–70
  Arguments for and against, 69
  The panel, 70
Metacognition, 8
Modelling facilitation, 9–10

Modulator, 9
Monitor, 9, 27

Narrative, 34, 35, 36, 37, 45, 47, 86
Narrative frameworks, 35–39
  Modern versions of fairy
    stories, 37
  Personal stories, 38–39
  Telling your own fairy stories,
    35–36
Negative responses, 29
News story, 50, 52, 54, 59, 60, 61

Observations of presenters sheet,
  55, 87
Opinion, 5, 23, 27, 28, 58, 59, 64,
  65, 69, 70, 74
Oral communication, 7
Oral presentation, 49

Pace, 40, 41, 87
Panel discussion, 70
Participation, 10, 27
Passion, 5
Peer/small-group assessment, 10
Performance skills, 40
Personal opinion/point of view,
  65–68
  Explaining my position, 65, 67
  Justifying an action, 68
  Presenting and contesting
    points of views, 66
  "What we believe"—Using
    supportive arguments, 65, 67
Personal stories, 38–39
Persuasion, 5, 64, 65, 73
Persuasive talk, 64, 65, 73
  Analyzing advertisement, 73
Pitch, 40, 41, 73, 87
PMI strategy, 14, 23
Point of view, 65, 66, 71, 75
Positive responses, 29
Presentation style, 55
Probing, 56, 59, 81

Proposed argument, 71
Provoker, 9, 27

Questioning strategies, 12, 29–30,
  57
Questions and interviews, 56–57
  Designing the questions, 57
  Identifying and using good
    questions, 56

Radio program assessment
  Mandatory roles, 61, 88
  Negotiable roles, 61, 89
Reading between the lines, 15
Recorder, 25
Reflective listening, 5–6
Reflective thinking, 27
Reflectiveness, 9
Reporter, 25
Reporting, 19, 49
Responsiveness, 9, 27
Risk taking, 9
Role of the teacher, 9, 27

Sample group interactive patterns,
  21
Scaffolding learning, 7, 9, 44
Self-assessment, 10, 49
Self-confidence, 5, 8
Shorts, 43
Small-group discussion, 20, 22, 37,
  40, 47, 54, 60, 61, 67, 70, 73, 74
Sociogram, 20, 21
Speaking skills, 7, 9, 10
Stereotyping, 36
Stimulating discussion, 32
Storyboards, 44
Story reading, 34
Story telling, 34, 38, 39, 40, 44,
  45–46, 48, 86
Strategies for engaging the
  audience, 40–47
  Chairs in pairs, 42
  Let me tell you a story, 45–46

Readers' theatre, 40
Shorts (30-second or one-
  minute presentations), 43
Telling the poem, 47
The town crier, 41
Using a storyboard, 44
Stress, 41
Structure of a debate, 74, 91
Student assessment, 10–11
Student profile assessment chart,
  32, 33, 48, 63, 75
Student-student interaction,
  20–24, 81, 85
Successful presentations, 43
Summarizing, 18, 19, 70
Supporter, 9

Teacher checklist for establishing
  a collaborative classroom, 11, 81
Thinking, 8
Timer, 25, 27
Tone, 73, 87

Using the skills, 59–60
  Creating news stories from
    pictures, 60
  Student reporters, 59

Volume, 40, 41
Voting criteria for a debate, 74, 92
Vygotsky, Lev, 5

Whole-class assessment, 10